# FAMILIARIZE ONESELF WITH EDUCATIONAL TECHNOLOGY

## KNOW SOMETHING INSIDE OUT

AF440730

HALLUR VIJAYALETCHUMY GANESH SANTHOSH SENTHIL

Copyright © Hallur Vijayaletchumy Ganesh Santhosh Senthil
All Rights Reserved.

This book has been self-published with all reasonable efforts taken to make the material error-free by the author. No part of this book shall be used, reproduced in any manner whatsoever without written permission from the author, except in the case of brief quotations embodied in critical articles and reviews.

The Author of this book is solely responsible and liable for its content including but not limited to the views, representations, descriptions, statements, information, opinions and references ["Content"]. The Content of this book shall not constitute or be construed or deemed to reflect the opinion or expression of the Publisher or Editor. Neither the Publisher nor Editor endorse or approve the Content of this book or guarantee the reliability, accuracy or completeness of the Content published herein and do not make any representations or warranties of any kind, express or implied, including but not limited to the implied warranties of merchantability, fitness for a particular purpose. The Publisher and Editor shall not be liable whatsoever for any errors, omissions, whether such errors or omissions result from negligence, accident, or any other cause or claims for loss or damages of any kind, including without limitation, indirect or consequential loss or damage arising out of use, inability to use, or about the reliability, accuracy or sufficiency of the information contained in this book.

Made with ♥ on the Notion Press Platform
www.notionpress.com

The most important thing to remember is that there is NO exact formula for writing a perfect dedication.Dedication is one of the most personal parts of your writing, and you are free to write it however you like.This book is especially dedicated to the teachers who helped and guided us to successfully complete this book work.Also I would like to dedicate this book to my dear father, who has been a wonderful supporter until my research was completed, and to my beloved mother, who has been encouraging me for months.We dedicate this Project to all the people who have worked hard to help us complete this book.

# Contents

# Foreword

In contemporary technology education, engineering design is becoming an essential component to connect technology with Science,Management, Mathematics, and Engineering. The engineering design process is an iterative process of devising a system, component, or strategy to meet desired needs. Still, there are many unanswered questions: "Why do we use the engineering design process?" "How do we use the design process?" and "How do students use the engineering design process to solve technological problems?" This chapter will review the existing engineering design process models presented by textbooks and researchers. Then, the author considers contemporary learning theories that align with the engineering design process in terms of design cognition. Next, the author will present a design process model derived from an experimental pattern study. This chapter will explain how students perceive and undertake the engineering design process in an authentic problem-solving setting, based on the research findings. Finally, this chapter contains practical suggestions on the use of the engineering design process in the classroom.

# Preface

Educational technology is the study and ethical practice of facilitating learning and improving performance by creating, using, and managing appropriate technological processes and resources. From the perspective of technology used in education, educational technology could be understood as the use of emerging and existing technologies to improve learning experiences in a variety of instructional settings, such as formal learning, informal learning, non-formal learning, lifelong learning, learning on demand, and just-in-time learning. Educational technology approaches have evolved from early uses of audiovisual aids to individual and networked computers, and now have evolved to include various mobile and smart technolo- gies, as well as virtual and augmented realities, avatar-based immersive environ- ments, cloud computing, and wearable and location-aware devices. Various terms have been used along the way to refer to educational technologies, such as learning technologies/environments and instructional technologies/systems. We have embraced a broad interpretation in this book to cover instructional design approaches, learning strategies, and hardware and software. Our view is that any- thing that consistently can support learning and instruction can be considered an educational technology. Some educational technologies are simple and have existed for many years; others are complex, and new ones are finding their way into educational settings every day.

Educational technology focuses on both the technical and pedagogical ways and means of supporting learning and instruction. It is the basis for the success of the e-learning revolution in recent years. Technology-based instruction can surpass traditional classroom-based instruction in quality by providing a wide variety of affordances and capabilities that can promote motivation and result in engaging, efficient, and effective learning.

The demand for educational technologies has been rising steadily; e-learning is a huge and expanding worldwide industry. Commercial e-learning companies, training departments in large companies and organizations, computer software companies, and educational institutions over the world employ large numbers of specialists in various aspects of educational technology creation (programming, graphic design, instructional design, task analysis, usability engineering, subject matter analysis, editing, etc.). However, these organizations often find it hard to employ suitably qualified workers who have knowledge beyond their subfields and disciplines. There is a strong demand for technologists who understand learning

theories and for instructional designers and educators who understand technologies and how to effectively integrate technology into learning and instruction. The field of educational technology is becoming part of major educational programs in institutions worldwide. The commercial training industry is large and still going through a period of rapid and sustained growth, based in large part on the inte- gration of advanced digital technologies.

The needs and requirements of the various organizations, both educational and commercial, vary widely in terms of the knowledge and skills needed to implement educational technology solutions effectively. Further complexity comes from the fact that potential students of educational technology exist at different levels and in a variety of contexts; potential students come from a variety of backgrounds, ranging from education, computing, engineering, design, arts, the humanities, finance, and the natural sciences. Their interests and expectations vary as widely as their aspirations toward what kind of organizations they would like to serve after their studies. The aim of this book is to prepare students with the knowledge and skills to understand the organizational needs and requirements, and not only use and manage existing and emerging technologies effectively, to be able to apply associated pedagogies and instructional strategies appropriately and effectively, to evaluate and manage edu- cational technology solutions, and to foresee and prepare for future possibilities.

This book is targeted toward readers who are interested in educational tech- nology and would like to understand educational technology from different per- spectives. Specifically, this book could be used as textbook for two types of undergraduate students: (a) those who are looking for careers in educational tech- nology, instructional design, or media and information systems, or may want to continue their studies in graduate programs in learning and instructional technology and (b) those who are interested in becoming teachers in K-12 settings or trainers in industry and who need a strong background in educational technology. This book will also act as a valuable resource in teacher education programs where the primary focus on mainstream education requires an authentic resource in instructional design and educational technology.

Keeping in mind the varied needs of the organizations, employees, and potential students, this book adopts a competency-based approach to learning and assess- ment. The themes and topics take a multi-disciplinary approach and are aimed at preparing students for competent and innovative educational technology profes- sionals. The approach taken in this book aligns with the recommendations of the suggested curricula for advanced learning technologies developed by a task force of the Institution of Electrical and Electronics Engineers' Technical Committee on Learning Technology.

# Acknowledgements

**Dr.Vishweshwarayya C Hallur**
**Professor | Innovator | Writer | Researcher**

It would not have been possible to write this book without the blessings of almighty. I praise God, the almighty for providing me this opportunity and granting me the capability to proceed successfully.I wish to sincerely thank all those who have contributed in one way or another to this study. Words can only inadequately express my deep gratitude to my mentor, Dr. Ravindra S. Hegadi, for his meticulous care, kindness and generosity.I must thank the management of Angadi Institute of Technology for their full support and encouragement while carrying out this book.I am extremely grateful to my parents for their love, prayers, caring and sacrifices for educating and preparing me for my future. I am very much thankful to my wife, my daughter and my son for their love, understanding, prayers and continuing support to complete this book. Also I express my thanks to my brothers and their family for their support and valuable prayers.

Thank you.

Dr. Vishweshwarayya C Hallur

# Acknowledgements

**Dr.VIJAYALETCHUMY SUBRAMANIAM**
**Professor | Innovator | Writer of author | Researcher**

I am forever indebted to my guiding spirit, Tan Sri Dato Dr. Syed Jalaluddin Syed Salim, who has always provided me with heartfelt support, invaluable guidance and inspiration. His unwavering support motivated me to further gain international expertise in dyslexia in Vancouver, Canada during my PhD.I am eternally grateful to my mentor,Prof. Datin Paduka Setia Dato' Dr. Aini Ideriswho taught me discipline, integrity,respect, and so much more that has helped me succeed in life. I truly have no idea where I'd be if she hadn't given me her support throughout. Also, my acknowledgement would not be complete without Assoc. Prof. Dr. Noor Aina Dani who chose me to be her next generation in the field of Malay language, especially in Psycholinguistics.Although this period of my life was filled with many ups and downs, my time in the industry would not have been made possible without my dear familywho has always been there for me. Special thanks to my husband, Elangkovan Muthu and my sons, Dr.NertiyanElangkovan, KaviyarasuElangkovan. I would also like to give my gratitude to my big family, my dear brothers and sisters. Mainly, my strength dear GunendranKrishnasamy who has always pushed me for the better in life.

**PROF. DR. VIJAYALETCHUMY SUBRAMANIAM**

# Acknowledgements

**Dr.GaneshKrish**
**Author | Innovator | Educator | career Architect**

Dr.Ganesh Krish,working at BSA Crescent University as a Director of placements, training, industry, and alumni relations. a professional with more than 20+ years of combined experience in education, training,Placement, Skill development, Manufacturing, International collaborations, Industry & Government Relations, SAP, software engineering in India and abroad.His Masters degrees include Business Management and psychology. He received his Hon.doctorate in Management & Sports Psychology, Employer Branding in campus placements. He has worked in industry and academia for more than 20+ years. Interactions between Institute, Industry and government are his main area of interest.He has won numerous honours, including the Best Placement Director Award and the Distinguished Innovative and Inspiring Academician Award. He has trained and placed more than 80K+ students across a range of businesses.He has published four books, four patents, and copyrights under his name.He is a professional cyclist who has achieved success internationally.

# Acknowledgements

Dr.K.SANTHOSH KUMAR
Professor/ Innovator/Writer of author/Researcher
    K.Santhosh kumar as born Byangi (village) in Tamil nadu in india 21 Dec 1985.He is received his B.Com(CA) : Sri Rama Krishna mission vidhyala , College of Arts and Science Coimbatore,Tamil nadu.He was received MCA Master of Computer Applications, Sri Rama Krishna Mission Vidhyala College of Arts and Science, Coimbatore ,He recived M.Phil Master of Philosophy in Computer Science,Rathnavel Subramaniam College of Arts and Science Coimbatore He received Ph.D (CS) Doctor of Philosophy in Computer Science,Rathnavel Subramaniam College of Arts and Science Coimbatore.In 2013 Hw joined in Assistant Professor the Department of Computer Science and Applications,Providence College for women,coonoor Tamilnadu.He is the visit Examinar various colleges and Schools.First of all I express my sincere thanks to Dr.Senthil my heartiest support and inspiring gudidance meticulous planning persistent efforts and fruitful discussion.Heartfelt thanks to my parents.

# Acknowledgements

**Dr.P.SENTHIL**

**Professor | Innovator | Writer of author | Researcher**

P.Senthil was born Varagubady(village) in Tamilnadu in India in 9 May 1987.He received his B.Sc., degree in Information Technology from Bharayhiyar University for coimbatore, Tamilnadu.He was received the M.Sc Information Technology and M.Phil degrees in Computer Science from Kurinji College Arts and Science,Trichy ,Tamilnadu in 2010, and 2014, respectively. In 2012, He joined in the Department of Computer Science,Kurinji College of Arts and Science in Trichy,Tamilnadu as a Lecturer and now He is working as Associate professor in the department of MCA, KCAS College of Arts and Science,Trichy Tamilnadu from June 2014 onwards. He is doing his research in Image mining & Digital Image processing at Bharathidasan University, Tamilnadu in India. He is the examination board member of various Colleges and Universities and He guided more than 6 MPhil Research scholars for various universities.He is 21 International Books published.

# Prologue

I observed a number of folks who were reluctant to share.

You who endure for me

If you choose not to bless me, I felt love.

I noticed a rampart; now is the moment to separate.

Before then, just light

Visual eyes

Fears the dark.

The thoughts travel back.

That will be seen in the distant one day.

Showing the chariot over the shoulder

I was unaware that you were the living god until I lifted.

A vertical mountain

I had forgotten that I was a conscious divinity until I met you.

You see, I refused to support God as my friend and protector.

Got up

Missing old pals

Father carried me as I felt

It seemed close to me.

The people that helped me as I You helped me when I was walking, therefore I offer my shoulder to assist the limping stride.

Only time will allow room in my heart to cleanse.

# Author Details


- Dr. Vishweshwarayya C. Hallur
  Associate Professor,
  Angadi Institute of Technology and Management, Belagavi-590009,
  Karnataka,INDIA

- Dr. Vijayaletchumy Subramaniam
  Professor of Applied Linguistics, University Putra Malaysia,
  43400 Serdang, Selangor Darul Ehsan,
  MALAYSIA.

- Prof. Dr. K. Ganesh Krish
  Director-Placement & Training.
  Industry & Alumni Relations
  B. S. A. Crescent Institute of Science & Technology
  GST Road, Vandalur, Chennai 600 048. Tamilnadu. INDIA

- Dr.K.Santhosh Kumar
  Assistant professor,Computer Science and Applications
  Providence College for women,Coonoor ,Tamil Nadu,INDIA

- Dr P.Senthil
  Associate Professor,Kurinji college arts and science,
  Tiruchirappalli -17 Tamilnadu,INDIA.

## CHAPTER ONE

# Introduction to Educational Technology

## Chapter Outline

- Introducing educational technology
- A brief history of educational technology
- The scope of educational technology
- Dimensions of educational technology
- Educational technology perspectives
- Emerging technologies and changing contexts
- Roles of educational technologists.

## By the End of This Chapter, You Should Be Able To

- Classify the key concepts and principles of educational technology
- Recall the history of educational technology
- Clarify the scope, dimensions, and perspectives of educational technology
- Reflect on the roles of educational technologists.

## Main Learning Activities

1. According to Merrill, Tennyson, and Posey, to teach a concept involves pointing out examples and non-examples, citing a rule or principle or criterion to distinguish examples from non-examples, and providing opportunities to prac- tice and get informative feedback. Given that context and the challenge to teach curious Cathy (an imaginary student) the concept "educational technology," cite three examples and three non-examples of educational technologies that you could show Cathy, and also provide a rule, principle, or criterion which she could use to distinguish the examples from the non-examples.
2. Select six additional items (some example and some non-examples), and ask Cathy to identify which are and which are not educational technologies. In each case, write down the formative and supportive feedback you would provide for both a correct and an incorrect response.
3. Suppose you are teaching a group of preservice teachers the first course on technology integration in learning and instruction and the first unit of instruction is on the history of educational technology.
4. List the topics and concepts that you would include in that unit of instruction. Provide several examples and explain why you would include them.

    a. List the resources that you would make available to those preservice teachers? Provide several examples and explain why you would include them.
    b. State the purpose, scope, objectives, and expected learning outcomes of that unit of instruction.
    c. Indicate how you would determine if the expected outcomes are achieved.
    d. Which pedagogical approach, instructional strategies, and technologies would you prefer to use and why?

6. Educational technology refers to the use of tools, technologies, processes, proce- dures, resources, and strategies to improve learning experiences in a variety of settings, such as formal learning, informal learning, non-formal learning, lifelong learning, learning on demand, workplace learning, and just-in-time learning. Edu- cational technology approaches evolved from early uses of teaching tools and have rapidly expanded in recent years to include such devices and approaches as mobile technologies, virtual and augmented realities, simulations and immersive environ- ments, collaborative learning, social networking, cloud computing, flipped class- rooms, and more. This chapter provides a historical overview, key definitions and principles, various perspectives and representative developments, all of which will be explored and elaborated in subsequent chapters.

7. The basic approach in this volume is competency-based. A competency is a collection of related knowledge, skills, and attitudes (KSAs) that enable a person to perform a particular task. There are many tasks that educational technologists perform as part of their role and responsibilities. This primer provides an elabo- ration of many of these tasks and the associated KSAs that are common in the twenty-first century, while building a grounded rationale for them on the basis of prior work in learning psychology, computer developments, and human–human and human–computer interaction.

8. Previous educational technology textbooks have focused primarily on knowl- edge and skills and have not emphasized attitudes and values as strongly as they are emphasized herein. The reason for emphasizing attitudes and values is that they play a critical role in motivation, and motivation is critical to success in nearly every human endeavor and especially critical in the challenging domain of edu- cational technology. The hope is that those who use this primer will develop an attitude exemplified by this statement: "I know we can improve learning, instruction and performance in this situation."

9. Stories and other forms of narrative can be useful in providing context as well as motivation. Here is a story that actually occurred.This story involves a middle school student (Charlie) who was blind and par- tially deaf from birth. Charlie wanted to learn to swim during his summer vacation. A volunteer high school student lifeguard agreed to work with this student over a two-month period, three days a week, an hour or two each day. The student life- guard was told that Charlie probably never would learn to swim but just being in the pool and doing something enjoyable would be good for him. The first week or two served to confirm that advice. Charlie enjoyed being in the cool water on a hot summer day and spent most of the time walking around in the shallow part of the pool, occasionally dunking his head under water with the help of the lifeguard.

10. After two weeks of getting used to being in the water, Charlie asked in difficult to understand broken words and gestures when he was going to learn to swim. Charlie wanted to swim. The lifeguard then decided to take Charlie's desire seri- ously, in spite of the parents saying not to try something so difficult for Charlie. The lessons started with kicking strokes with Charlie holding on to the edge of the pool and the lifeguard holding Charlie in a horizontal position. The following week, this was practiced in deeper water away from the edge of the pool. At the end of the first month, Charlie had learned how to say afloat for a few minutes by kicking his legs while in a vertical position in deeper water, with the lifeguard nearby to encourage him. The adult supervisor of the swimming lessons was somewhat surprised at Charlie's progress and encouraged the lifeguard to continue.

11. To shorten the story, at the end of the second month, Charlie was able to swim, somewhat awkwardly, from one side of the pool to the other—not the length of the pool, just the width which was about 10 m. The last day involved the parents of the children who had been taking swimming lessons. Charlie's parents came and were amazed to see him swim the width of the pool, which was something that no one really thought he would be able to do. Sometimes, one can do more than is expected by others. In this case, the local swimming community including the lifeguard and swimming supervisor supported Charlie's strong desire to learn to swim.

12. The point of this story is to emphasize the role that *desire* plays in achieving outcomes. Desires need to be heard, accommodated, and supported to the extent that is reasonable in a given situation. From the instructor's perspective, the rele- vant attitude was to help the learner, Charlie, achieve his goal. Teachers and trainers can help learners develop an appropriate attitude—in this case, the desire to master.

## CHAPTER TWO

# Learning in the Context of Technologies

**Chapter Outline**

- Behaviorism
- Cognitivism
- Constructivism
- Other learning theories
- Technology-enhanced learning.

**By the End of This Chapter, You Should Be Able To**

- Clarify the background and main ideas of different learning theories
- State the relationship of technology and learning theories
- Describe the impact of learning theories on teaching, including behaviorism, cognitivism, constructivism, connectivism and humanism

**Main Learning Activities**

1. Think about what is learning and the advantages and disadvantages of program instruction and discuss with your peers.
2. Think about the characteristics and functions of sensory memory, short-term memory, and long-term memory as well as the implications of information processing theory for instruction. More specifically, how would you characterize your response to the discussions of behaviorism and cognitivism? Were you passive as a reader or were you processing what you read and creating ideas or cognitive structures?
3. Think about what are the differences between individual/cognitive construc- tivism and social constructivism? In addition, think about the implications of constructivism for teaching.
4. Think about the implications of connectivism for teaching. Suppose you want to learn more about climate change, who might you ask to gain a better under- standing? Is there a group you might join to follow up on your interest?
5. Think about the integration of technology and education and how the learning theories evolved over time. Do you find a connection between specific tech- nologies and learning theories? Can you describe a couple of examples?
6. Work with your group members or peers, to create a concept map to show how learning theories and technologies are related to each other. Modify the concept map based on your discussion in the group.

# Linking Learning Objectives, Pedagogies, and Technologies

**Chapter Outline**

- Linking instructional strategies to learning objectives
- Types of technology for educational uses
- Principles for the selection of technology for educational uses.

**By the End of This Chapter, You Should Be Able To**

- Differentiate types of learning objectives;
- Select an appropriate instructional strategy for a given learning objective;
- Identify the types of pedagogical approaches and associated technologies to suit particular types of learning.
- Provide advice on how to match types of pedagogical approaches and technologies to types of learning.

**Main Learning Activities**

1. Think about what kind of pedagogies that have been mentioned in this chapter that impact the selection of appropriate technologies. What other pedagogies can be added in the selection of appropriate technologies? What pedagogical approach has been used in this chapter? What additional strategies and tech- nologies would you recommend to go with this chapter in a classroom setting?
2. Suppose you are planning to teach an 8-grade student about ocean tides (or another learning task of your choosing). Identify an appropriate learning objective for a lesson about ocean tides. Then indicate an appropriate peda- gogical approach to support that objective. Next, consider affordable tech- nologies that could be used to support such a lesson.

## CHAPTER FOUR

# Users Perspective of Educational Technology

**Chapter Outline**

- User experience
- User-centered design
- Learner-centered design
- The ARCS Model of motivational design.

**By the End of This Chapter, You Should Be Able To**

- Define user experience and user-centered design
- Differentiate user-centered design and learner-centered design
- Recall the honeycomb model for designing user experience and the ARCS model of motivational design
- Clarify the processes and principles of user-centered design
- Provide advice on how to involve users in the design and how to carry out learner-centered design.

**Main Learning Activities**

1. Think about why user experience (UX) should be considered for educational technology system and products, and what kind of components should be taken into consideration to design UX for educational technology system and products? Give specific examples.
2. Think about what you will do step by step to design an educational technology product, like an APP? Try to use a specific example even if is imaginary. For example, you might use a critical thinking game for kids as the example.
3. Think about the users for one educational technology product; if the product can be redesigned, what suggestions can you provide for designers to improve the product by involving users? When and how would you recommend involving them?
4. Think about differences between users and learners? Consider this in terms of a specific technology. What are their different perspectives? How to consider learners' special needs in designing an educational technology system? You might use a product such as Microsoft Word to illustrate your ideas.
5. Think about what is the differences between user and learner motivation in using a specific product. Describe the product and specific uses. How can one go about considering a variety of user and learner needs in designing an educational technology system?

## CHAPTER FIVE

# Learner Experiences with Educational Technology

**Chapter Outline**

- Experience and learner experience
- Elements of learner experience with educational technology
- Indicators to evaluate learner experience.

**By the End of This Chapter, You Should Be Able To**

- Describe general experience and learner experience
- Define learner experience and characterize varieties of learner experience
- List and elaborate the elements of learner experience
- Describe indicators of and their use in analyzing learner experience.

**Main Learning Activities**

1. Think about what constitutes learner experience and why learner experience is important for educational technology. How would you characterize your experience in reading this chapter? What might be done to improve your learning experience with regard to this chapter?
2. Think about what element is most important for a meaningful learner experience. Which element of this chapter has been most meaningful to you? Why? Of the five elements discussed above, which of them can you identify in this chapter?
3. Choose a type of educational technology according to four categories (tools, resources, environments, and methods) of the educational technology discussed in this chapter. Pick a technology with which you are familiar. Identify the elements of the learner experience involving educational technology and also indicate relevant principles to guide design, development, and effective use of the technology.

## CHAPTER SIX

# Social Learning Perspective of Educational Technology

**Chapter Outline**

- Social learning
- Features of technology in social learning
- Building learning communities/group
- Analysis and measure group learning.

**By the End of This Chapter, You Should Be Able To**

- Clarify the definition of social learning
- Build and manage a learning community
- Conduct interaction analysis through social network analysis and content analysis method.

**Main Learning Activities**

1. According to your own experience, describe a social learning experience and your own perceptions as well as summarize the advantages of social learning. Think about what are the differences among a social learning approach, behavioral, and cognitive approaches.
2. Describe a learning community with which you have been involved and state what makes a learning community. You can use this class as an example if you have no other option.
3. Think about why technology is essential in social learning. What kind of roles technology can play to promote social learning, and describe a social learning scenario for the applied technology?
4. Think about how to build and manage learning group in a classroom if you are a teacher?
5. Think about how to measure group learning performance. What kind of com- ponents should be considered? Do think how to measure and evaluate group work in this course?

## CHAPTER SEVEN

# Designing Learning Activities and Instructional Systems

**Chapter Outline**

- Learning activity design
- Bloom's taxonomy
- Cognitive load theory
- Mayer's principles of multimedia learning
- Instructional Systems Design.

**By the End of This Chapter, You Should Be Able To**

- Identify and describe learning activity design and instructional design.
- Classify Bloom's taxonomy.
- Clarify the principles of multimedia learning.
- Reflect on a learning activity design.

**Main Learning Activities**

1. Identify and describe how to get students engage in the materials without the traditional face-to-face interaction, and indicate what kinds of additional sup- ports should be considered to make the best case for your solution approach. Create a concept map that reflects the things indicated in response to the pre- vious content.
2. Using Bloom's taxonomy of learning, locate where instructional design might fall and explain why.
3. Which of Gagné's nine events of instruction might be associated with the scaffolding method in cognitive apprenticeship and how so?
4. Describe a typical instructional flow for a small unit of instruction such as a single lesson, including the knowledge and learning objects involved along with activity, sample feedback, and assessment.
5. Explain what you will do when you do a learning activity design if you con- sidering cognitive load theory?
6. Talk about what you will do when you design a multimedia learning resource by considering Mayer's cognitive theory?
7. Explain the process of designing a course by applying the ADDIE model.

# Learning Space Design

**Chapter Outline:**

- Definition of learning space
- PST framework
- Principles for learning space design
- Smart learning environment.

**By the End of This Chapter, You Should Be Able To**

- Recognize differences in informal and formal learning
- Define a learning space
- Understanding Pedagogy-Space-Technology design and evaluation framework
- Recall the principles of learning space design
- Clarify the element and technique features of smart learning environment
- Elaborate on two examples of learning space design.

**Main Learning Activities**

1. Take a few minutes to describe a particular learning space with which you are familiar. What pedagogical approach is used in that space? What technologies are involved? Is the space suitable for that pedagogical approach and those technologies? Explain why or why not.
2. Create a concept map that depicts the key features of a learning space. Describe a specific learning space for a formal learning situation and also one for an informal learning space. State what is needed to make each example a smart learning space.

## CHAPTER NINE

# Educational Project Design and Evaluation

## Chapter Outline

- Character of Educational projects
- Life cycle of educational projects
- Logic model for educational project design
- CIPP model for educational project evaluation.

## By the End of This Chapter, You Should Be Able To

- Identify the life cycle of educational projects
- Clarify the processes of educational project design
- Use logic model to design educational projects
- Use CIPP model to evaluate educational projects.

## Main Learning Activities

1. In your own words, state what is meant by educational projects and cite two specific examples.
2. Describe an educational project with which you have been involved and say what kind of work you did.
3. Describe the steps you might use to address the problem of an educational project in the example you have just described.
4. Use the life cycles of educational project to explain the example you found in learning activity 1. Indicate similarities and differences with regard to the instructional design process discussion in a previous chapter.
5. Use the educational project design logic model to design an educational project to fix the problem of low performance of students in math. Situation: In one math class, 60% of the students are sleeping, 20% of the students are following teacher, 20% of the students are playing with their phones, and teacher is reading the textbook.
6. Think about the relation among main factors in logic model and in CIPP model. Explain the difference between outputs and outcomes. Which of those two is directly linked to goals and objectives?

## CHAPTER TEN

# Design-Based Research

**Chapter Outline**

- Characters of design-based research
- The process of design-based research
- DBR and traditional empirical research methods.

**By the End of This Chapter, You Should Be Able To**

- Clarify the characteristics of design-based research
- Use design-based research (DBR) to design research procedures
- Identify the differences of DBR and traditional empirical research methods.

**Main Learning Activities**

1. Think about when one would do design research and how to do a design-based research in educational technology. Try to think of such an effort in the context of a specific technology-based implementation.
2. After you learn the characters and process of DBR (design-based research), please draw a mind map to illustrate the relationships between the key steps of DBR. Please discuss with your peers about the differences of DBR and the traditional predictive research methods. When you are carrying out educational technology research, what methods will you use and why?

# Design Methodology

**Chapter Outline**

- The framework of design methodology
- Original requirements analysis
- Target user analysis
- Stakeholder analysis
- Competitor analysis

**By the End of This Chapter, You Should Be Able To**

- Scenario analysis
- Function list
- Identify and describe design methodology;
- Understand the framework of design methodology;
- Use design methodology for educational product.

**Main Learning Activities**

1. Draw a mind map to express the key processes of design methodology.
2. Think about how to design an educational product and the challenges of implementing design methodology in education/game creation.

## CHAPTER TWELVE

# Emerging Issues in Educational Technology

**Chapter Outline**

- Emerging technologies in education
- Issues involving in emerging technologies
- Challenges for educational technology.

**By the End of This Chapter, You Should Be Able To**

- Identify the essential technologies in technology.
- Identify immerging issues when using technology.
- Identify seven challenges for educational technology and some recommenda- tions to meet the challenges.

**Main Learning Activities**

1. Discuss with peers on the emerging technologies for education, and describe what do you think the future leaning and teaching will be?
2. Discuss with peers on the issues of using technology in education, and list all the items you mentioned.
3. Describe a specific example of integrating an emerging technology into a unit of instruction.
4. State the rationale for using that technology and indicate how its impact on learning will be determined. Note likely issues to arise in making effective use of the new technology in an actual learning setting.

# The Scope Of Educational Technology

**Introduction**

Learning is a process that brings together personal and environmental experiences and influences for acquiring, enriching or modifying one's knowledge, skills, values, attitudes, behaviors, and worldviews. Learning theories develop hypotheses that describe how this process takes place. The scientific study of learning started in earnest at the dawn of the twentieth century. Behaviorism, cognitivism, socio-constructivism, and other views have been proposed as the emphasis has been placed on cognitive style and emerging educational technologies. These theories will be discussed in subsequent sections.

In this chapter, firstly the definition of learning in the context of technologies will be described. Then, learning theories, including behaviorism, cognitivism, constructivism, and other views, will be discussed. Finally, technology-enhanced learning will be described briefly and elaborated in subsequent chapters.

Learning happens everywhere and everyday for everybody, but what is learning? Most people have the intuition that learning implies the ability to do something that the learner could not do before or know something that the learner did not know before.

In most psychological theories, learning is defined as a persistent change in human performance or performance potential. According to Spector, the changes could include one's abilities, attitudes, beliefs, knowledge, and skills. However, the major concepts and principles of learning vary with learning theories in different ages. Learning theories are conceptual frame- works describing how knowledge is absorbed, processed, and retained during learning. In the process of designing and developing instructional

systems, learning environments and learning activities relevant learning theories and psychological perspectives include behaviorism, cognitivism, constructivism, connectivism, and humanism.

**Behaviorism**

Behaviorism was elaborated by Watson, among others. Watson was an American psychologist whose research was published in the early part of the twentieth cen- tury. Behaviorism was dominant in American psychology for half a century from the 1920s to the 1960s and remains one of the most important schools of American psychology. The main representatives of behaviorism include John B. Watson (1878–1958), Burrhus F. Skinner (1904–1990), and Edward L. Thorndike (1874– 1949).

**Main ideas**

Behaviorism is a perspective that focuses almost exclusively on directly observable things to explain learning. That which is directly observed and believed most relevant to learning are the immediate things in the learner's environment, and most closely contiguous in time and place to the targeted learning— the so-called *stimulus* conditions for learning. The *response* of the learner to the stimulus is also directly observable and serves as an indicator of learning.

The major idea of behaviorism includes the following:

- The learning process is a gradual attempt and error until the consistent success is attained.
- The key to learning success depends on reinforcement.
- Learning involves a stimulus–response sequence.

Edward L. Thorndike (1905) developed an stimulus–response (S-R) theory of learning. In stimulus–response theory, knowledge is defined as a learner's collec- tion of specific responses to stimuli that are represented in behavioral objectives (Koehler & colleagues). Edward L. Thorndike noted that responses (or behavior) were strengthened or weakened by the consequences of behavior: (1) a response to a stimulus is reinforced when followed by a positive rewarding effect, and (2) a response to a stimulus becomes stronger by exercise and repetition. Different reinforcement patterns (i.e., continuous or intermittent) have been shown to have a different impact on learning outcomes (Ferster & Skinner).

Behaviorism puts emphasis on the importance of the environment during indi- vidual learning. According to behaviorism theory, teaching is to control the learning environment to achieve the desired results, and the main method of controlling learning behavior is to strengthen the correct response. Behaviorism pioneer, Watson said, Give me a dozen healthy infants, well-formed, and my own specified world to bring them up in and I will guarantee to take any one at random and train him to become any type of specialist I might select – doctor, lawyer, artist, merchant-chief and, yes, even beggar-man and thief, regardless of his talents, penchants, tendencies, abilities, vocations, and race of his ancestors. I am going beyond my facts and I admit it, but so have the advocates of the contrary and they have been doing it for many thousands of years (Watson).

### The impact on teaching

Burrhus F. Skinner proposed *operant conditioning.* Operant conditioning is a type of learning in which the strength of a behavior is modified by the behavior's consequences, such as reward or punishment. In operant conditioning, stimuli are present when a behavior is rewarded or punished to control that behavior. For example, a child may learn to open a box to get the candy inside, or learn to avoid touching a hot stove; the box and the stove are discriminatives.

According to operant conditioning, the probability of the behavior occurring in this scenario is enhanced by the reinforcement. Learning is understood as the step-by-step or successive approximation of the intended partial behaviors by the use of reward and punishment.Programmed instruction is based on Skinner's operant conditioning. It is a method of presenting new subject matters for students in a graded sequence of controlled steps.

- According to programmed instruction, the textbooks are divided into small frames and small steps, and each frame has its own goals. Learners could achieve their goals through certain learning procedures.
- Students work through the programmed material by themselves at their own speed. After each step, we can test their comprehension by answering an examination question or filling in a diagram. They are then immediately shown the correct answer or given additional information.
- Instruction is self-paced, and learners are required to be active by completing exercises and tests and proceeding based on feedback from the instruction.

The learning essence of behaviorism is the change of the external behavior caused by the environment. Impacts on teaching are that the desired results could be achieved through controlling the learning environments, while the main measures of control learning include present stimulus, provide practice, feedback and rein- forcement, such as strengthening the correct response.

### Cognitivism

Cognitivism psychology was initiated in the late 1950s and became dominant in the late 1970s and the early 1980s. The main representatives include Jean Piaget (1896–1980), Jerome S. Bruner (1915–2016), David P. Ausubel (1918–2008), and Robert M. Gagné (1916–2002), among others.

Cognitivism arose within psychology as behaviorism was proved to be insuffi- cient to explain complex human learning, such as language learning. In order to explain some human behaviors, psychologists turned to investigate the information processing in the mind which is considered as unobservable black box by behav- iorists. People are no longer viewed as collections of responses to external stimuli as understood by behaviorists, but as information processors.

### Main ideas

In cognitive psychology, learning is conceptualized as the acquisition of knowledge: The learner is an information processor who absorbs information, undertakes cognitive operations on it, and stocks it in memory.

According to cognitivism, learning is not a stimulus–response sequence, but the formation of cognitive structures. The learners do not simply receive stimuli mechanically and react passively, but, rather, learners process stimuli and determine appropriate responses.

Cognitivism has its roots in cognitive psychology and information processing theory. The best way to introduce cognitivism is through Anderson's ACT-R model of information processing Information processing theory involves how people receive, store, integrate, retrieve, and use information. The basic idea of the information processing theory is that the human mind is like a computer or information processor.

This model proposes that information is processed and stored in three stages: sensory memory, short-term memory, and long-term memory. They are assumed to receive information from environment and transform it for storage and use in memory and performance.

- A learner's environment activates the receptors (sense), and information is then transmitted through the sensory memory to short-term memory in selected and recognizable patterns (7 plus or minus 2 chunks of information). The infor- mation is held in short-term memory for about 20–30 s (unless rehearsed), and then, the information to be acquired is transformed by a process known as semantic encoding to a form that enters long-term memory (Cognitivism and Gagne's Model of Learning). With sensory memory, learners perceive organized patterns in the environment and begin the process of recognizing and coding these patterns.
- Short-term memory (working memory) permits the learner to hold information

briefly in mind to make further sense of it and to connect it with other infor- mation that is already in long-term memory.

- Long-term memory enables the learner to remember and apply information long after it was originally learned.

### Impact on teaching

As a cognitive psychologist, Gagné proposed nine events of instruction and conditions of learning as effective means to activate and support the processes of information processing shows these instructional events in the left column and the associated internal mental process in the right column.

The impact on teaching from cognitivism is as the following:

1. In the design of computer-aided instruction, people began to pay attention to the internal psychological process of learners and then began to study and emphasize the learners' psychological characteristics and cognitive structures.
2. Educators no longer regard learning as the learner's passive response to external stimuli, but consider learning as involving attitudes, needs, interests, hobbies, and cognitive structures.
3. The teacher's task is to try to arouse the learners' interest and motivation and then combine the current teaching content with the original knowledge and experience of the learners.

### Constructivism

Constructivism emerged in the 1970s and 1980s as an extension of cognitivism that included an emphasis on internal mental constructions and the influence of others on an individual's learning. The main ideas are based on the works of John Dewey (1859–1952) and Lev Vygotsky (1896–1934).

### Main ideas

Constructivism holds that learning is the process of constructing internal psycho- logical representation in the process of the interaction with the environment. Helping learners involves helping them to understand the nature, regularity, and the inner connections among things. The basic elements of con- structivism include context, collaboration, conversation, and meaning-making.

**From constructivism, learning could be understood in the following ways.**

1. Learning is or should be learner-centered.
2. Learning is the process by which learners construct internal psychological representation actively.
3. The learning process consists of two aspects: the reorganization and recon- struction of old knowledge and the meaningful construction of new knowledge.

4.  Learning is not only an individualized behavior, but also a social and language-centered behavior; learning requires communication and cooperation.
5.  Learning involves emphasizing the situation of learning and attaching impor- tance to the creation of meaningful situations to support learning.
6.  Effective learning requires appropriate resources to support meaning construction.

### The impact on teaching

According to constructivism, teachers should not teach in the traditional way, but should encourage students to cooperate or interact with peers. Students should process information and construct meaning of knowledge actively, rather than listen to teachers passively. The impact of constructivism on teaching is as follows:

1.  Pay attention to the design of learning scenario. The teacher should design multi-dimensional learning scenarios, so that learners can understand the concept of principles from various aspects, and then develop problem-solving, decision-making, and innovation capabilities.
2.  Emphasize the learner's active role. Focus on cultivating students' self-management skills to stimulate the necessary psychological state and prior knowledge for learning.
3.  Pay attention to the contribution of error concept to learning. Situated cog- nition theory treats the aim and process as unity. Therefore, even the erroneous concept being produced in the process of learning, it also has a positive contribution to the construction of the whole knowledge structure.

### Social constructivism

Constructivism can be viewed simply as individual/cognitive constructivism, whereas social constructivism recognizes the role of language and others in learning. The main idea is that learning is a meaning construction process. The individual constructivism is mainly developed on the basis of Piaget's thoughts. According to Piaget's theory of cognitive development, learning is the process by which learners form, enrich, and adjust their cognitive structures through the interaction of new and old knowledge and experiences. The two main cognitive processes involved are assimilation (using an existing mental construct or schema in a new situation) and accommodation (altering an existing schema or creating a new one based on a new situation).

The main representative of social constructivism is Lev Vygotsky. Vygotsky's social constructivist theory highlights the following aspects:

1.  Social and cultural interactions play a very important role in the learning process.
2.  Knowledge is co-constructed and that individuals can learn from one another.
3.  The learner must be engaged in the learning process. Learning happens with the assistance of other people.

Based on the research of the socio-constructivism, puts for- ward the Zone of Proximal Development (ZPD). This is a "range of tasks that are too difficult for an individual to master alone, but can be mastered with the assis- tance or guidance of adults or more-skilled peers." Another part of this theory is scaffolding, which emphasizes to give the learner the right amount of assistance at the right time. If the learner can perform a task with some assis- tance, then he or she is closer to mastering it. These theories have an important influence and enlightenment on teaching, and some new teaching methods have formed, such as anchored instruction, cooperative learning, and reciprocal instruction.

### Main ideas

Connectivism is a hypothesis of learning which emphasizes the role of social and cultural context. It is the integration of principles from chaos, network, and com- plexity and self-organization theories. The central aspect of connectivism is the metaphor of a network with nodes and connections. In this metaphor, a node is anything that can be connected to another node such as an organization, information, data, feelings, and images. In this sense, connectivism proposes to see knowledge's structure as a network and learning as a process of pattern recognition.

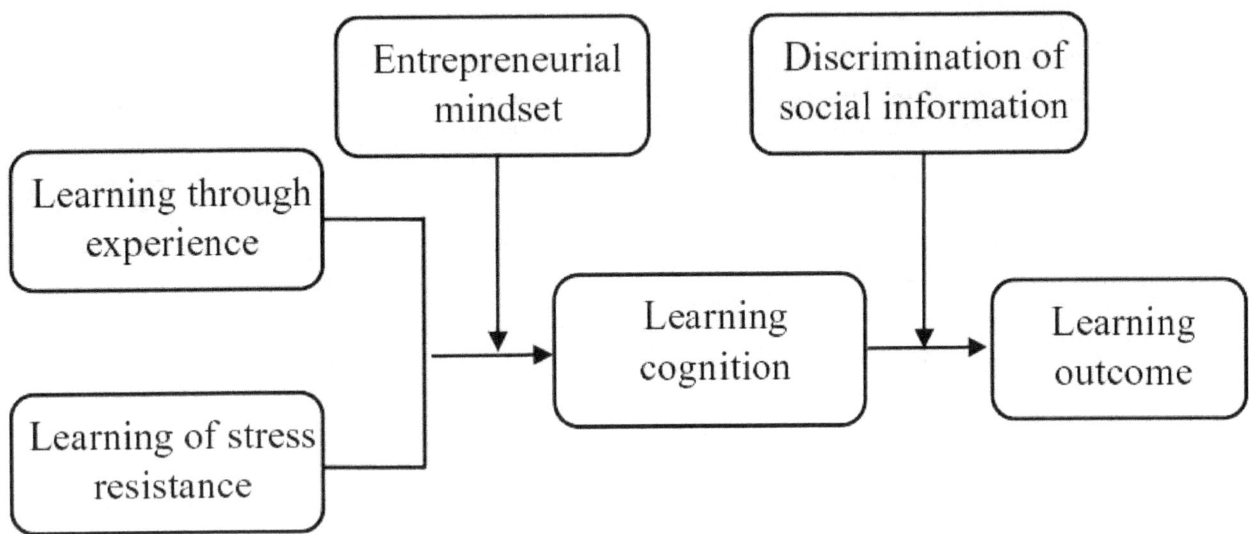


Fig 2.1:Learning is creating networks

According to connectivism, learning is creating networks (Fig.2.1). Nodes are external entities, which can be used to form a network. The nodes may be people, organizations, libraries, Web sites, books, database, or any other source of infor- mation. The act of learning is creating an external network of nodes, where we connect information and knowledge sources. The learning that happens in our heads is an internal network (neural). Learning networks can then be perceived as structures that we create in order to stay current and continually acquire experience, create, and connect new knowledge (external). Learning networks can be perceived as structures that exist within our minds (internal) in connecting and creating pat- terns of understanding.

**Other Learning Theories**

Besides behaviorism, cognitivism, and constructivism, there are many other learning theories, which play an important role in guiding teaching and learning activities, such as connectivism and humanism.

Learning is a process that brings together personal and environmental experiences and influences for acquiring, enriching or modifying one's knowledge, skills, values, attitudes, behaviors, and worldviews. Learning theories develop hypotheses that describe how this process takes place. The scientific study of learning started in earnest at the dawn of the twentieth century. Behaviorism, cognitivism, socio-constructivism, and other views have been proposed as the emphasis has been placed on cognitive style and emerging educational technologies. These theories will be discussed in subsequent sections.

In this chapter, firstly the definition of learning in the context of technologies will be described. Then, learning theories, including behaviorism, cognitivism, constructivism, and other views, will be discussed. Finally, technology-enhanced learning will be described briefly and elaborated in subsequent chapters.

Learning happens everywhere and everyday for everybody, but what is learning? Most people have the intuition that learning implies the ability to do something that the learner could not do before or know something that the learner did not know before.

In most psychological theories, learning is defined as a persistent change in human performance or performance potential. According to Spector, the changes could include one's abilities, attitudes, beliefs, knowledge, and skills. However, the major concepts and principles of learning vary with learning theories in different ages. Learning theories are conceptual frame- works describing how knowledge is absorbed, processed, and retained during learning. In the process of designing and developing instructional

systems, learning environments and learning activities relevant learning theories and psychological perspectives include behaviorism, cognitivism, constructivism, connectivism, and humanism.

### Behaviorism

Behaviorism was elaborated by Watson, among others. Watson was an American psychologist whose research was published in the early part of the twentieth cen- tury. Behaviorism was dominant in American psychology for half a century from the 1920s to the 1960s and remains one of the most important schools of American psychology. The main representatives of behaviorism include John B. Watson (1878–1958), Burrhus F. Skinner (1904–1990), and Edward L. Thorndike (1874– 1949).

### Main ideas

Behaviorism is a perspective that focuses almost exclusively on directly observable things to explain learning. That which is directly observed and believed most relevant to learning are the immediate things in the learner's environment, and most closely contiguous in time and place to the targeted learning— the so-called *stimulus* conditions for learning. The *response* of the learner to the stimulus is also directly observable and serves as an indicator of learning.

**The major idea of behaviorism includes the following:**

- The learning process is a gradual attempt and error until the consistent success is attained.
- The key to learning success depends on reinforcement.
- Learning involves a stimulus–response sequence.

Edward L. Thorndike (1905) developed an stimulus–response (S-R) theory of learning. In stimulus–response theory, knowledge is defined as a learner's collec- tion of specific responses to stimuli that are represented in behavioral objectives (Koehler & colleagues). Edward L. Thorndike noted that responses (or behavior) were strengthened or weakened by the consequences of behavior: (1) a response to a stimulus is reinforced when followed by a positive rewarding effect, and (2) a response to a stimulus becomes stronger by exercise and repetition. Different reinforcement patterns (i.e., continuous or intermittent) have been shown to have a different impact on learning outcomes (Ferster & Skinner).

Behaviorism puts emphasis on the importance of the environment during indi- vidual learning. According to behaviorism theory, teaching is to control the learning environment to achieve the desired results, and the main method of controlling learning behavior is to strengthen the correct response. Behaviorism pioneer, Watson said,Give me a dozen healthy infants, well-formed, and my own specified world to bring them up in and I will guarantee to take any one at random and train him to become any type of specialist I might select – doctor, lawyer, artist, merchant-chief and, yes, even beggar-man and thief, regardless of his talents, penchants, tendencies, abilities, vocations, and race of his ancestors. I am going beyond my facts and I admit it, but so have the advocates of the contrary and they have been doing it for many thousands of years (Watson, p. 82).

The impact on teaching Burrhus F. Skinner proposed *operant conditioning.* Operant conditioning is a type of learning in which the strength of a behavior is modified by the behavior's consequences, such as reward or punishment. In operant conditioning, stimuli are present when a behavior is rewarded or punished to control that behavior. For example, a child may learn to open a box to get the candy inside, or learn to avoid touching a hot stove; the box and the stove are discriminative stimuli.

According to operant conditioning, the probability of the behavior occurring in this scenario is enhanced by the reinforcement. Learning is understood as the step-by-step or successive approximation of the intended partial behaviors by the use of reward and punishment.

Programmed instruction is based on Skinner's operant conditioning. It is a method of presenting new subject matters for students in a graded sequence of controlled steps.

- According to programmed instruction, the textbooks are divided into small frames and small steps, and each frame has its own goals. Learners could achieve their goals through certain learning procedures.
- Students work through the programmed material by themselves at their own speed. After each step, we can test their comprehension by answering an examination question or filling in a diagram. They are then immediately

shown the correct answer or given additional information (The Columbia Encyclope- dia).

- Instruction is self-paced, and learners are required to be active by completing exercises and tests and proceeding based on feedback from the instruction.

The learning essence of behaviorism is the change of the external behavior caused by the environment. Impacts on teaching are that the desired results could be achieved through controlling the learning environments, while the main measures of control learning include present stimulus, provide practice, feedback and rein- forcement, such as strengthening the correct response.

### Cognitivism

Cognitivism psychology was initiated in the late 1950s and became dominant in the late 1970s and the early 1980s. The main representatives include Jean Piaget (1896–1980), Jerome S. Bruner (1915–2016), David P. Ausubel (1918–2008), and Robert M. Gagné (1916–2002), among others.

Cognitivism arose within psychology as behaviorism was proved to be insuffi- cient to explain complex human learning, such as language learning. In order to explain some human behaviors, psychologists turned to investigate the information processing in the mind which is considered as unobservable black box by behav- iorists. People are no longer viewed as collections of responses to external stimuli as understood by behaviorists, but as information processors.

### Main ideas

In cognitive psychology, learning is conceptualized as the acquisition of knowl- edge: The learner is an information processor who absorbs information, undertakes cognitive operations on it, and stocks it in memory.

According to cognitivism, learning is not a stimulus–response sequence, but the formation of cognitive structures. The learners do not simply receive stimuli mechanically and react passively, but, rather, learners process stimuli and determine appropriate responses. Cognitivism has its roots in cognitive psychology and information processing theory. The best way to introduce cognitivism is through Anderson's ACT-R model of information processing Information processing theory involves how people receive, store, integrate, retrieve, and use information. The basic idea of the information processing theory is that the human mind is like a computer or information processor.

This model proposes that information is processed and stored in three stages: sensory memory, short-term memory, and long-term memory. They are assumed to receive information from environment and transform it for storage and use in memory and performance.

- A learner's environment activates the receptors (sense), and information is then transmitted through the sensory memory to short-term memory in selected and recognizable patterns (7 plus or minus 2 chunks of information). The infor- mation is held in short-term memory for about 20–30 s (unless rehearsed), and then, the information to be acquired is transformed by a process known as semantic encoding to a form that enters long-term memory (Cognitivism and Gagne's Model of Learning). With sensory memory, learners perceive organized patterns in the environment and begin the process of recognizing and coding these patterns.
- Short-term memory (working memory) permits the learner to hold information briefly in mind to make further sense of it and to connect it with other infor- mation that is already in long-term memory.
- Long-term memory enables the learner to remember and apply information long after it was originally learned.

### Impact on teaching

As a cognitive psychologist, Gagné proposed nine events of instruction and conditions of learning as effective means to activate and support the processes of information processing shows these instructional events in the left column and the associated internal mental process in the right column.

The impact on teaching from cognitivism is as the following:

1. In the design of computer-aided instruction, people began to pay attention to the internal psychological process

of learners and then began to study and emphasize the learners' psychological characteristics and cognitive structures.

2. Educators no longer regard learning as the learner's passive response to external stimuli, but consider learning as involving attitudes, needs, interests, hobbies, and cognitive structures.

3. The teacher's task is to try to arouse the learners' interest and motivation and then combine the current teaching content with the original knowledge and experience of the learners.

### Constructivism

Constructivism emerged in the 1970s and 1980s as an extension of cognitivism that included an emphasis on internal mental constructions and the influence of others on an individual's learning. The main ideas are based on the works of John Dewey (1859–1952) and Lev Vygotsky (1896–1934).

#### Main ideas

Constructivism holds that learning is the process of constructing internal psycho- logical representation in the process of the interaction with the environment. Helping learners involves helping them to understand the nature, regularity, and the inner connections among things. The basic elements of con- structivism include context, collaboration, conversation, and meaning-making.

From constructivism, learning could be understood in the following ways.

1. Learning is or should be learner-centered.
2. Learning is the process by which learners construct internal psychological representation actively.
3. The learning process consists of two aspects: the reorganization and recon- struction of old knowledge and the meaningful construction of new knowledge.
4. Learning is not only an individualized behavior, but also a social and language-centered behavior; learning requires communication and cooperation.
5. Learning involves emphasizing the situation of learning and attaching impor- tance to the creation of meaningful situations to support learning.
6. Effective learning requires appropriate resources to support meaning construction.

#### The impact on teaching

According to constructivism, teachers should not teach in the traditional way, but should encourage students to cooperate or interact with peers. Students should process information and construct meaning of knowledge actively, rather than listen to teachers passively. The impact of constructivism on teaching is as follows:

1. Pay attention to the design of learning scenario. The teacher should design multi-dimensional learning scenarios, so that learners can understand the concept of principles from various aspects, and then develop problem-solving, decision-making, and innovation capabilities.
2. Emphasize the learner's active role. Focus on cultivating students' self-management skills to stimulate the necessary psychological state and prior knowledge for learning.
3. Pay attention to the contribution of error concept to learning. Situated cog- nition theory treats the aim and process as unity. Therefore, even the erroneous concept being produced in the process of learning, it also has a positive contribution to the construction of the whole knowledge structure.

#### Social constructivism

Constructivism can be viewed simply as individual/cognitive constructivism, whereas social constructivism recognizes the role of language and others in learning. The main idea is that learning is a meaning construction process. The individual constructivism is mainly developed on the basis of Piaget's thoughts. According to Piaget's theory of cognitive development, learning is the process by which learners form, enrich, and adjust their cognitive structures through the interaction of new and old knowledge and experiences. The two main cognitive processes involved are assimilation (using an existing mental construct or schema in a new situation) and accommodation (altering an existing schema or creating a new one based on a new situation).

The main representative of social constructivism is Lev Vygotsky. Vygotsky's social constructivist theory highlights the following aspects:

1. Social and cultural interactions play a very important role in the learning process.
2. Knowledge is co-constructed and that individuals can learn from one another.
3. The learner must be engaged in the learning process. Learning happens with the assistance of other people.

Based on the research of the socio-constructivism, puts for- ward the Zone of Proximal Development (ZPD). This is a "range of tasks that are too difficult for an individual to master alone, but can be mastered with the assis- tance or guidance of adults or more-skilled peers." Another part of this theory is scaffolding, which emphasizes to give the learner the right amount of assistance at the right time. If the learner can perform a task with some assis- tance, then he or she is closer to mastering it. These theories have an important influence and enlightenment on teaching, and some new teaching methods have formed, such as anchored instruction, cooperative learning, and reciprocal instruction.

**Main ideas**

Connectivism is a hypothesis of learning which emphasizes the role of social and cultural context. It is the integration of principles from chaos, network, and com- plexity and self-organization theories. The central aspect of connectivism is the metaphor of a network with nodes and connections. In this metaphor, a node is anything that can be connected to another node such as an organization, information, data, feelings, and images. In this sense, connectivism proposes to see knowledge's structure as a network and learning as a process of pattern recognition.

According to connectivism, learning is creating networks (Fig.2.1). Nodes are external entities, which can be used to form a network. The nodes may be people, organizations, libraries, Web sites, books, database, or any other source of infor- mation. The act of learning is creating an external network of nodes, where we connect information and knowledge sources. The learning that happens in our heads is an internal network (neural). Learning networks can then be perceived as structures that we create in order to stay current and continually acquire experience, create, and connect new knowledge (external). Learning networks can be perceived as structures that exist within our minds (internal) in connecting and creating pat- terns of understanding.

**Other Learning Theories**

Besides behaviorism, cognitivism, and constructivism, there are many other learning theories, which play an important role in guiding teaching and learning activities, such as connectivism and humanism.

**Connectivism**

Over the last twenty years, technology has changed how we live, how we com- municate, and how we learn. With the development of the information technology, such as social networking and cloud computing, connectivism has been put forward and gained increasing attention. The main representatives include George Siemens and Stephen Downes.

**Humanism**

Humanism emerged in the 1950s and became popular after the 1960s. Humanistic psychologists believe that the school should integrate the concept and practice of moral education into various teaching activities and help the students to develop a sound personality. The main representative includes Abraham Maslow (1908– 1970) and Carl Rogers (1902–1987).

**Main ideas**

Humanism is a perspective that focuses on the value of the individual and personal freedom. According to humanism, each person has the ability to develop his or her own potential and motivation. Individuals can freely choose their own development direction and value. Humanism focuses on human's overall development, empha- sizes human dignity and value, and pays attention to the health and integrity of people. Humanism investigates mainly how to create a good environment for learners to perceive the world from their point of view and develop an under- standing of the world, aiming to achieve the highest level of self-realization.

Over the last twenty years, technology has changed how we live, how we com- municate, and how we learn. With the development of the information technology, such as social networking and cloud computing, connectivism has been put forward and gained increasing attention. The main representatives include George Siemens and Stephen Downes.

### Humanism

Humanism emerged in the 1950s and became popular after the 1960s. Humanistic psychologists believe that the school should integrate the concept and practice of moral education into various teaching activities and help the students to develop a sound personality. The main representative includes Abraham Maslow (1908– 1970) and Carl Rogers (1902–1987).

### Main ideas

Humanism is a perspective that focuses on the value of the individual and personal freedom. According to humanism, each person has the ability to develop his or her own potential and motivation. Individuals can freely choose their own development direction and value. Humanism focuses on human's overall development, empha- sizes human dignity and value, and pays attention to the health and integrity of people. Humanism investigates mainly how to create a good environment for learners to perceive the world from their point of view and develop an under- standing of the world, aiming to achieve the highest level of self-realization.

The scope of educational technology is quite large as it involves the application and practice of using technologies (in the form of tools, techniques, resources, pro- cesses, etc.) to support, facilitate, and enhance learning, performance, and instruction. While educational technology has emerged as a recognized discipline and profession in the last 50 years, it is a dynamic, complex, and interdisciplinary enterprise. It is dynamic in part due to the rapid changes occurring in technology. It is complex due to the many interacting factors, components, and people involved in an education system or learning environment; moreover, many of the relationships among those factors, components, and people are nonlinear and change over time. Educational technology is inherently an interdisciplinary enterprise involving,among others, content experts, technical specialists, teachers, and administrators, who have different backgrounds and formal training. For an elaboration of a cur- riculum for advanced learning technology.

For the instructor: Before discussing education systems, consider a class dis- cussion on the notion of a person as a system—that is to say, a collection of related and interacting components with different kinds of relationships among those components. Consider identifying subsystems and discussing one or more of those in some detail. If possible, identify delayed effects within the human system as well as nonlinear relationships among some of the components.

One way to elaborate the scope of educational technology is to consider the life cycle of a representative education system or learning environment. First, consider that you have vacation time coming and you and your family are discussing where to go and what to do on the vacation. How might that discussion proceed? You might begin with wishes and desires, or you could begin with constraints (time, money, distance, etc.). Either way, the discussion has to start somewhere and both kinds of considerations are relevant—desires and constraints. In a sense, both of those considerations are likely to narrow the choices. At some point, the discussion might involve specific activities or sites or experiences that could become the basis for some consensus. Each person involved is voicing a point of view and expressing an opinion. In such a situation, it is quite natural to include those involved in the discussion to ensure that the vacation will be as successful as possible. Compro- mises are likely to occur as the discussion evolves. When a decision is reached, it might then be desirable to distribute the various tasks associated with implementing the decision (e.g., making reservations, collecting and packing appropriate clothes, notifying friends). Keep vacation planning in mind as a model as the much more complex enterprise of educational technology planning is elaborated.

For the sake of this discussion, let us suppose that a new course has been mandated for all high school students namely formal and informal logic. There is no requirement to have any knowledge about the subject of logic to follow this discussion. Indeed, an educational technologist recruited to support the effort might well have no subject matter knowledge at all. How might the process evolve? The sections that follow indicate some of the concerns, questions, activities, and pro- cesses that might be part and parcel of the life-cycle planning and support of this course from the perspective of educational technology. It is worth noting [and probably worth discussing/challenging in class] that some form of technology is involved in nearly every course, so this discussion naturally involves educational technology. The perspective represented below is not necessarily what is typical when a new course is being planned. In many cases, the content expert or teacher is the primary person leading the way. However, the more that technology is critical for the effort and the larger the scale of the effort, the more important it is that educational technologists and instructional designers play leading roles.

**Needs Assessment**

How to begin planning support for a new course in formal and informal logic for high school students? Let us suppose that you, the educational technologist in the role of instructional designer, are at the initial planning meeting for this effort, along with a logic teacher, a school administrator, and a system specialist. The admin- istrator begins by stating the mandate—namely, create a new course on formal and informal logic and implement it using the school's learning management system, since the course will be conducted entirely online anytime in the student's last two years, at the students' pace, and required for graduation.

The logic teacher is excited that the subject is receiving such special treatment. You are concerned, however, about the rationale and motivation for the course. You ask, "Who decided that this should be done? How was the need determined? What problem are we trying to solve?" The administrator is prepared and offers the results of a study of graduates and their successes and failures over a five-year period. The administrator called this an exploratory effort to find out how well graduates were doing. As it happened, the study showed that of the 73% of graduates who went directly to college, 57% of them dropped out during the first two years. Surveys suggested that most of those who dropped out felt unprepared for the rigors of college. Follow-up interviews suggested that the lack of preparation involved the challenges of thinking critically and logically required in many of the college courses. You respond by saying that it was wise to conduct that study, which is one kind of needs assessment. The study in effect identifies a gap in high school education. Those in the room readily agree that this gap exists and that it should be addressed.

This example shows a progression from a symptom (high school students entering college drop out at a high rate) to a problem (a gap in preparing high school students to think critically and logically) to a need (address that gap with a new course aimed at developing general reasoning skills). A needs assessment is a way to identify symptoms and likely underlying causes resulting in a clear and coherent statement of the problem to be addressed. It is important to spend time and effort in determining the problem and associated need to avoid unnecessary rework or solving the wrong problem. The remaining life-cycle aspects will be addressed in turn, as this discussion is intended to be introductory and notional. Special emphasis has been placed on needs assessment as that is a critical first step.

**Requirements and Feasibility Analysis**

Once the problem and need have been identified, the goal or goals of the effort can be identified. These goals also form the basis for determining the degree to which the effort is succeeding once a solution is developed and deployed. It is now possible to begin considering solution approaches and a solution. This can and should be done with the desired goals in mind, as that is how the solution will be

**The Scope of Educational Technology**

In this case, it was determined that there was no room in the daily schedule of courses conducted in the school setting for a new course. The school happened to have an online learning management system, and the system administrator indicated that it could be used to host a new course. The logic teacher indicated that the content could be delivered online, including practice with feedback, although the formal tests should take place in a monitored situation at the school. Two tests were proposed, one for the first half of the course on formal logic and a second one for the second half of the course on informal logic. Both tests had to be passed in order to pass the course. Passing would involve a grade of 80% or better on each test, with possibilities for remediation and retesting.

It seems that many decisions had already been made prior to bringing the educational technologist on board. This is not so unusual and has led one of the authors to specify the Universal Underlying Principal of all Systems (including education systems; UUPS pronounced "oops" Something has already gone wrong. When a project begins and the educational technologist joins the effort, it is not uncommon for the educational technologist to believe that a bad decision has already been made. Sometimes, it is due to the lack of a needs assessment (not so in this case). In other cases, it is due to a particular solution or solution approach being mandated that is not necessarily an optimal way to address the problem. Perhaps having a self-paced online course with automated feedback on progress and little or no collaboration is not what you believe best in this case, so you raise the question why that particular approach while recognizing the need to offer the course online and outside the normal day-to-day schedule? The administrator then responds that doing it as a self-paced online course with automated feedback will allow it to be offered to other students not at this school who sign up at a cost. Doing it that way can generate revenue for the school.

You then note that this was not part of the identified need or problem being addressed. In a way, this is what planners and implementers call *mission creep* expanding the scope of the effort as it evolves. The first corollary to UUPS is that mistakes and oversights rarely occur alone; one often leads to another. You point this out to the administrator and say that there then needs to be added a second need generating revenuealong with a second goal and outcome measure.

When asked if you can design and develop such a course in collaboration with the content expert, you say you believe so, but you will need to learn more from the content expert and the system administrator. That follow-on deliberation can be considered an early feasibility review of the requirements now in place. Once a simple prototype is constructed early in the design process, a more robust feasibility study can be conducted to confirm that what has been planned can indeed be accomplished.

For the learner: Three corollaries to UUPS have been identified: (1) Mistakes rarely occur in isolation; one tends to lead to another; (2) resources are nearly always inadequate to do what you believe should be done; (3) others generally have good ideas. Were any of these corollaries evident in the example of creating a new online logic course? If so, describe how. If not, indicate how they might have been brought into that discussion.

**Design/Redesign:**Designing and planning learning activities, selecting and sequencing resources, creating units of instruction, and determining formative and summative assessments are typical tasks to be accomplished as a course is being designed. The big three issues for those planning and implementing courses are: (a) What to teach (content to be learned), (b) how to teach (strategies and activities to promote understanding and mastery), and (c) how to identify things to do differently (evaluation of the course with the potential to improve subsequent versions).

To guide these activities, it is useful to have an overall approach in mind along with associated instructional strategies. At this stage, very close collaboration with the context expert is required. While the content expert is likely to understand what is to be learned very well, it is not as likely that a content expert will understand how best to promote the desired learning. Determining the assumptions being made by the content expert is important as some of those assumptions might require confirmation or turn out be without foundation. Moreover, a content expert will often have a desire to do much more than can be realistically accomplished and may well have a different goal in mind than the one established at the beginning. For example, a content expert may unwittingly want students to become dedicated scholars in that subject area, which was not the original goal. Keeping focused on the goal and desired outcomes is an ongoing challenge. A creative educational technologist can elicit from content expert ideas about innovative activities and learning experiences tightly connected with the specific goals of the effort.

Content experts have a tendency to include the full breadth and depth of their knowledge, while an educational technologist or instructional designer is generally trained to stay close to activities, content, and resources directly aligned with desired learning outcomes. Awareness of these different perspectives is important. The attitude of a content expert might be expressed in this way: "I want my students to love this subject area just like I do." On the other hand, the attitude of the educational technologist might be expressed as follows: "I want students to succeed in attaining the targeted learning outcomes."

There are many approaches that can be used in a course. In the logic course case, the overall approach has been partially predetermined—namely a self-paced online approach with primary interactions taking place between an individual learner and the learning system. Within that general approach, there are opportunities for a variety of instructional strategies, ranging from a didactic and expository strategy (present content, provide practice cases with feedback, quiz, etc.) to a problem-based strategy (start with problems and have the learner explored the resources to find a solution). There are also variations of how much learner control to include and when it is desirable to include learner control of such things as

### The Scope of Educational Technology

Problems, topics, resources, and so on. Finding an approach that best fits a situation is a typical challenge for an educational technologist.Many important decisions occur during the planning or design phase, and it is desirable to see what others think about those decisions. Another corollary to UUPS is this: Others frequently have good ideas. In this case, a second content expert might be invited to offer a perspective and students who have had a similar course could be invited to offer a student perspective. Since the course is being designed to help high school graduates succeed in their first few years at college, it might also be good to involve college instructors who have lots of students dropping out due to poor reasoning capability. Because part of the design process involves selecting resources and activities, prior to fully developing those resources and activities it might also be wise to have input with regard to the meaningfulness and appro- priateness of those things. Finally, part of the design process involves specifying how the user interface will work, so having input on the interface in terms of usability and learnability prior to committing resources to development is also a good idea.

During the design phase of an effort, or sometimes earlier, it is generally a good idea to create an implementation plan to guide development and deployment and an evaluation plan that includes both formative and summative evaluations. Many funded efforts require that such plans are submitted with a project proposal.

### Development

Once a design has been specified, it is possible to begin developing and imple- menting the course. The implementation plan can guide this process. This devel- opment process is likely to involve the content expert and a number of specialists (e.g., a media specialist, a programmer, and a system specialist). By this point in the development of the course, a number of constraints probably had to be addressed and compromises made, which should be documented. Another UUPS corollary is that resources are seldom adequate to do what you and team believe should be done. Compromises are often necessary. However, what should rarely be com- promised is the intended goal of the effort.

Since a number of highly trained people are involved, it is again wise to proceed in steps, beginning with a working prototype that includes parts of all major components including the interface. Once such a working prototype has been developed, it can be tested internally, just as the design was tested one or more times before being passed on to development. This iterative process of design and development is sometimes referred to as design research. This iterative process of refinement can continue into the deployment phase as data on use by students become available.

A point worth emphasizing is that each of these activities is seldom a one-time-and-done kind of thing. It may happen in the evolution of the logic course that the automated feedback mechanisms are not working as they should, or perhaps the system is losing track of learner progress through the various modules. Any number of problems with the implementation can be discovered and addressed during development. A variety of educational technologists are likely to be involved during development (see the roles of educational technologists below). Coordinating their various efforts is a challenging task and one that best resides with the lead educational technologist or instructional designer (not the content expert nor the system administrator).

### Deployment

Prior to full-scale deployment on a school-wide or larger basis, it is generally wise to try out the course with a small but representative group of students, including both high-performing students and those who are not doing as well. It is likely that such a trial field test will result in a need to make changes in the design and/or the development of the course. Again, this is a step in a design research approach and it should be well documented, as should each step in this evolving process.Finally, the course goes live. Is the work of educational technology now done in this case? If you said yes, do not pass, go, or leave the room—there is much more work yet to be done.

**For the learner:** What else do you think needs to be done for the newly created logic course to be considered a success?

### Management

It is likely that the emphasis will shift from the educational technologist to the system administrator and the content expert who will monitor progress and report problems back to the educational technology team should they occur. Plans should be made to (a) monitor student progress, (b) gather and report student performance outcomes, perceptions, and reaction, and (c) track students subsequent to gradua- tion. In some cases, it is required to have a management plan in place; for large-scale efforts, such a plan is advisable even if it is not required.

### Evaluation

Once the course is deployed, the natural question to address is whether or not it is achieving its intended goals. To what extent are goals being met? That question is what drives a summative evaluation of the effortor periodic summative evalua- tions of the effort. It was mentioned earlier that documenting the effort as it was being designed, developed, and deployed was important. That documentation and associated observations and interviews with key persons as the effort evolves constitute what can be considered a formative evaluation of the effort, again con- sistent with a design research approach. It is often difficult to interpret the findings of an impact study or summative evaluation without the results of a formative evaluation. An evaluation plan typically includes a formative evaluation plan (e.g., a fidelity of implementation study that typically documents progress and includes interviews and observations) and a summative evaluation plan (e.g., an impact study). As mentioned previously, an evaluation plan is often developed early in the effort. In this case with the online logic course aimed at improving reasoning skills to help high school graduates succeed in college, the impact study needs to involve graduates several years after they have completed the new course.

### Support

Support for an educational technology effort runs throughout the process. Deter- mining support requirements and needs occurs early in the process. Identifying key personnel and training them begin early and continue throughout design, devel- opment, and deployment. Educational technologists as well as system specialists, programmers, and various staff are likely to be involved in providing support for the online logic course. Students need to know whom to call when they encounter problems. In this case, if the problem involves logic and solving problems, then a tutor might need to be identified and trained.

### Training

As previously suggested, identifying training needs and then helping prepare and implement training materials and sessions are important in ensuring the success of an innovative educational technology project. Tutors and staff support personnel obviously need to be trained in order to properly support the new course. Moreover, training students in the first week or so of the course might be required in order to ensure that students know what is expected and can perform all of the necessary actions and activities required in the course. Many innovative educational tech- nology projects fail due to poor communication and inadequate preparation and training of key personnel.Not only is educational technology a multi-disciplinary enterprise but is also multifaceted, having a number of dimensions to take into consideration in light of the processes discussed above and the roles to be discussed below. One of the things that makes educational technology such an interesting profession is the diversity of people, problems, needs, technologies, and solutions that are involved. If one thrives on challenges and complexity, then educational technology is well worth pursuing.

Hartley and colleagues conducted a three-year study aimed at developing a curriculum for advanced learning technology. Among the dimensions of practice and scholarship relevant to the field, they cited the following:

- Computer and software architecture and engineering
- Design research
- Human–computer interaction
- Learning psychology
- Program evaluation

- Project management
- Social interactions
- System thinking.

Another way of conceptualizing the dimensions of this complex and multi-disciplinary discipline is in terms of the activities, processes, and things with which educational technologists are commonly involved, as in the following brief overview.

### Communication/Coordination

When conducting the research to establish competencies for professionals involved in various aspects of educational technology, the International Board of Standards for Training, Performance and Instruction (ibstpi) found that the most critical skill area was communication communication competency includes oral, written, and aural skills as well as the ability to make an effective use of various communication modalities and representation forms. Along with effective communication skills are associated coordi- nation skills (e.g., collaborating, compromising, managing, leading). Unfortunately, very little effort is placed on developing communication and coordination skills in many academic programs where the emphasis tends to be on mastering the subject matter. We consider it a myth that people are born with a golden tongue or gift of gab or leadership skills. Those skills can be trained and developed and are among the competences recommended for those being trained as advanced learning technologists.

### Content/Resources

With the advent of the Internet, the resources that educational technologists and content experts can access for inclusion in a learning environment are enormous. One way to capture the complexity of this dimension is in terms of a hierarchy that begins with information resources at the base of a pyramid. Infor- mation that has been determined to be reliable and accurate can be considered knowledge and a candidate for inclusion among learning resources. When that knowledge is linked to a learning goal or objective, it can be considered a learning resource. When activities, feedback, and assessment are included with a learning resource, it becomes an instructional object or resource.

### Hardware Devices and Software

In addition to having to deal with so many learning resources, educational tech- nologists have to be familiar with, understand, and/or manage a wide variety of devices and associated software. If one focuses only on a computer to be used as the primary delivery or support device, then there are still many things to take into account, including a variety of workstations, personal computers, tablet computers, handheld computers, and so on with various operating systems, software, network configurations, cloud-based systems, and more. One might say that the price of competence as an educational technologist is nearly constant professional devel- opment. Openness to new possibilities created by the affordances of new and emerging technologies is required for an educational technologist to maintain currency and relevance as a professional practitioner.

### Implementation

Educational technologists not only need to know about and understand how people learn and the resources and devices that can support learning, they need to know how to do a variety of things to make support for learning real and effective. In some cases, this may take the form of transferring a reliable text-based resource into a visual form. In other cases, it may require the inclusion of support for discussion forums and chat rooms. In still other cases, support may require the collection and analysis of learner actions and inputs. In a general way, educational technologists need to understand what teachers, students, and support personnel do in order to provide appropriate tools and technologies to help make them more effective and productive in their various activities. An interesting in-class or online activity or discussion could involve a response to these questions:

(a) What kinds of learning experiences exist? (b) Who are involved in supporting learning? (c) What kinds of things can be done using technology to support all those involved in learning, performance, and instructional activities?

### Media and Representation Formats

Along with the explosion of resources available on the Internet have come a wide variety of representation formats. As the educational technology timeline suggests, text, pictures, audio, and video occurred were dominant in the nineteenth century and first half of the twentieth century. Within each of those media categories, there were a variety of types, such as black and white photographs, graphs along with text, and so on. With the advent of computing and the Internet, the ways and means of representing knowledge resources grew dramatically. Perhaps, a dramatic way to represent the rich variety of representation formats is with the painted scroll from the Song dynasty called ".The Web site shows a progression of replicas of the original scroll that was more than 5 m in length, culminating with an electronic animated 3D version that is more than 150 m in length and put on display in 2010 at the Shanghai Expo.

### Educational Technology Perspectives

As previously referenced, the work by Hartley and colleagues on developing a curriculum for the broad domain of advanced learning technologies resulted in important foundation work pertaining to understanding the knowledge, skills, and competencies required of educational technologies. Their work involved numerous surveys of professionals and academics, a detailed review of the research and practice literature, interviews, and focus group discussions over a three-year period. Because the goal was to create a curriculum framework, it was deemed appropriate to adopt a competency framework. As results were compiled, five clusters of related competencies emerged: Knowledge competence domain—as should be obvious at this point in the discussion, an educational technologist has to have well-developed knowledge in a number of areas, including learning psychology, human–computer inter- action, social psychology, instructional design, software engineering, technology integration, and so on.

1. Process competence domain understanding what is possible with regard to a variety of devices and software is critical for an educational technologist; main- taining an up-to-date understanding of what can and cannot be done and at what cost and with which expertise is expected of an educational technology professional.
2. Application competence domain educational technologists are often respon- sible for *making things happen*, such as taking the specification for a learning environment or course and translating that specification into a reality; that ability requires competence in a number of application areas, including the creation of media resources and assessment mechanisms.
3. Personal and social competence domain the work of educational technologists offers within the context of a team involving persons with different backgrounds and expertise; as previously indicated, effective communication, collaboration, and coordination skills are critical for success as a professional practitioner.
4. Innovation and creativity competence domain new technologies and approa- ches to learning create a need for professionals to be flexible and creative in making use of appropriate resources and technologies to achieve desired out- comes; this often involves significant changes in learning activities, teaching methods, and instructional designs.

### Emerging Technologies and Changing Contexts

One of the basic beliefs guiding this volume involves change. Learning is char- acterized by stable and persisting changes in what a person or group of people know and can do. Monitoring changes and progress of learning is among the things that educational technologists need to understand, as do teachers and learners. Tech- nologies change, as indicated in the earlier discussion of the history of educational technology. Changes in technologies are occurring at an increasing rate, as noted previously. In addition, there are changes in how formal learning is conceptualized and organized. The world of the educational technologist is dominated by change, and the various things that change have an effect on each other. A new technology can introduce a new approach to teaching. Subsequent chapters in this volume will revisit the impact of these changes on learning, performance, and instruction. An excellent source for information about emerging technologies and their likely impact on learning and instruction is the New Media Consortium and their annual *Horizon Reports* in a variety of locations and contexts. As an advance organizer for subsequent chapters, a few remarks on emerging technologies and changing contexts follow.

### Emerging Technologies

What are some of the emerging technologies? In the category of devices and hardware, 3D printers and wearable computing devices come to mind. Three-dimensional printers are already having an impact associated with a movement called makerspace, in which learners engage in using a 3D printer to create and test an object or artifact in the context of learning by doing and design-based learning. Wearable devices such as smartwatches and Internet-enabled head-mounted dis- plays exist and will surely find their way into a variety of learning and instructional situations.

In the category of processes and applications of advanced technologies, learning analytics, adaptive instructional systems, and personalized learning are being tested in small-scale situations as extensions of earlier intelligent tutoring systems that can take into account a robust and dynamic representation of the learner in terms of prior knowledge and performance, interests, motivation, preferences, and even moods. Game-based learning, gamification, and augmented and virtual realities are among the emerging technologies that are gradually finding their way into learning and instructional situations. It is nearly impossible to envision all of the possible technologies likely to emerge in the next 10 years. What is certain is that there will be many and the challenge of being a competent educational technologist will increase, along with the need for increasing refined areas of specialization and expertise.

### Changing Contexts

What is the likely impact of new and emerging technologies on learning and instructional contexts? Some envision a world in which everyone has access to the collected knowledge and wisdom of humanity along with automated learning and instructional devices and mechanisms; some even predict the disappearance of schools and teachers in such a world. We do not share that particular vision of the future, although we clearly acknowledge that formal learning environments are changing along with increased informal learning resources and environments. An obvious change in formal contexts involves the rapid growth of online learning. Hybrid learning environments that integrated online resources and activities with face-to-face contexts are now the norm in many higher educational institutions as well as in some K-12 schools. Because there are so many Internet resources available to so many people, often at no cost, many teachers are now adopting the practice of flipping the classroom. This involves assigning readings and associated discussions outside of class, sometimes within an Internet-based environment, and using class time to have students practice applying knowledge learned outside class on problems, sometimes working in small groups. This allows the teacher to shift the role from primary presenter of information to that of providing constructive and meaningful feedback to develop learner competence and enhance the application and transfer of knowledge to solving meaningful problems.Other changes are occurring as well.

Whereas literacy used to focus on reading, writing, and basic arithmetic, the concept of literacy has expanded considerably to include digital literacy, which includes multiple literacies (e.g., information literacy, technology literacy, visualization literacy). This means that the notion of basic skills typically taught in primary and secondary school settings has been enlarged, and supporting the development of digital literacy skills using technology is one obvious approach.

Pedagogical approaches are also changing. Since the introduction of interactive simulations in the last part of the previous century, there has been a growing emphasis on learning by doing, sometimes also referred to as authentic or situated learning. Augmented and virtual realities and immersive environments have sig- nificantly enhanced the power of interactive simulations. As a result, such appli- cations are expected to continue to change and influence how knowledge and expertise are developed.

### Roles of Educational Technologists

Those trained in the area of educational technology end up in various professional positions with a variety of responsibilities. What follows is a brief review of the job titles, roles, and responsibilities associated with educational technology profes- sionals; it is not intended to be a complete or comprehensive of the various roles in which educational technologists are placed.

- Instructional designer responsible for planning, analyzing, designing, devel- oping, modifying, implementing, evaluating, and/or managing a variety of courses, instructional systems, and learning environments

- Instructional project manager responsible for leading instructional development projects, directing educational programs, and/or managing the creation of learning environment efforts
- Media specialist responsible for creating, finding, modifying, and/or using a variety of media artifacts in various formats
- Technology coordinator responsible for helping teachers and instructors find, modify, use, and/or integrate a variety of educational technology resource
- System administrator responsible for managing and supporting an education system, content management system, learning management system, and/or a network environment used to support learning and instruction Developer/programmer—responsible for coding instructionally related softwareand/or developing mediated objects and resources to be used in support of learning and instruction.
- Evaluator responsible for the formative and summative evaluation of lessons, courses, programs, instructional systems, and/or learning environments

- Instructor responsible leading units of instruction, tutoring students, and/or providing learning guidance and feedback in the context of formal learning contexts.

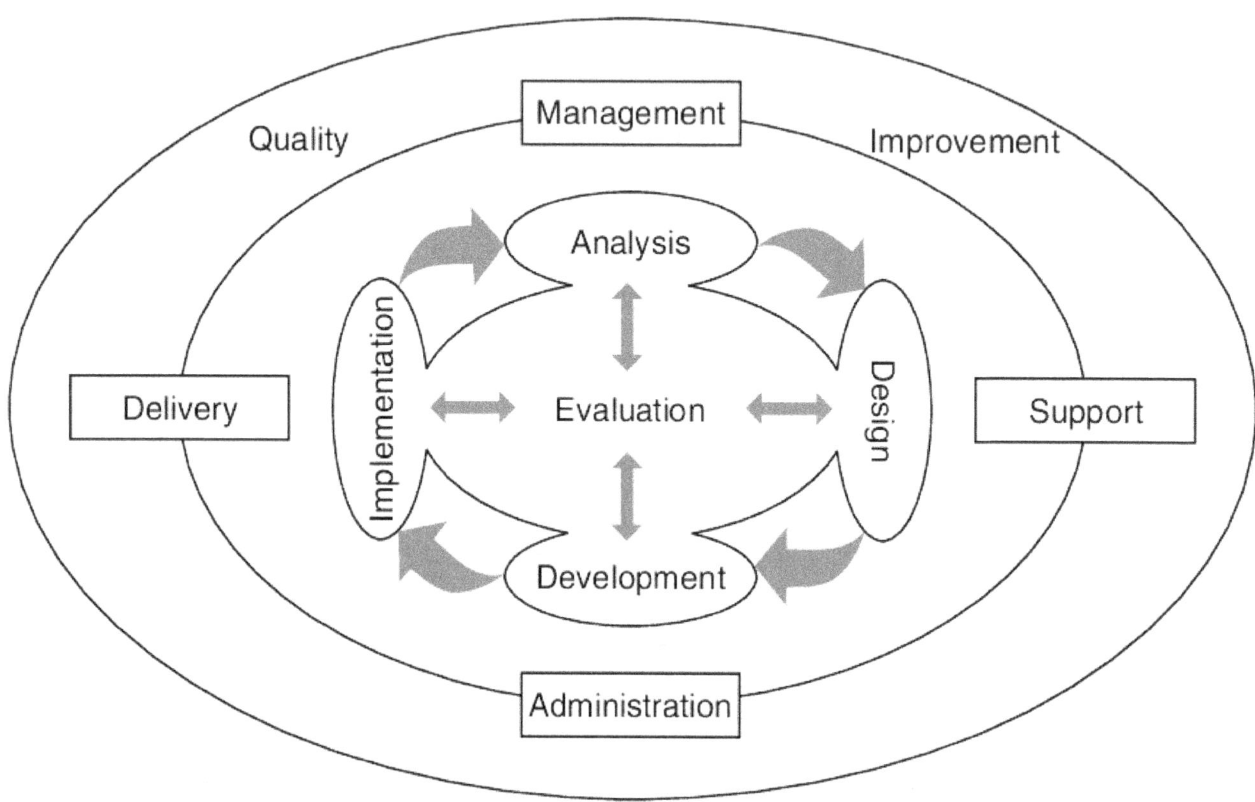


Fig 2.1 Fourth-Generation Instructional Systems Development

Another way to represent the complexity of educational technology is in terms of Robert Tennyson's Fourth-Generation Instructional Systems Development (ISD) model (see Fig.2.1). Note that in this context, the notion of "development" covers the entire life cycle of planning, implementing, managing, and evaluating an educational effort. Some practitioners refer to this notion of development as big D, and some also use design in the same big D sense to cover the entire life cycle. In this volume, we generally use design and development to refer to specific tasks rather than the entire process.

Terminology is often an important component of gaining competence in a particular domain. For that reason, we have included definitions of key terms in each chapter in an effort to use those terms as would most educational technologists. Nonetheless, different uses do occur in various situations. That is particularly true with regard to terms "assessment" and "evaluation" which are treated later in this volume. In general, and by way of an advance organizer, "assessment.

**Roles of Educational Technologists**

Technology used to refer to individuals learners or workers. "Evaluation" on the other hand is most often used to refer to courses, projects, programs, products, policies, pro- cesses, or practices. There are two things especially noteworthy in Tennyson's ISD model. First, a situational evaluation applies regardless of where in that model one happens to be working. Second, the model is elaborate primarily in terms of what people do. As a consequence, that model can serve as a point of departure for elaborating in more detail the roles of an instructional designer, which are differ- ently defined than those of an educational technologist.

**Key Points in This Chapter**

1. AECT definition of educational technology is the study and ethical practice of facilitating learning and improving performance by creating, using, and managing appropriate technological processes and resources.
2. The scope of educational technology includes needs assessment, requirements and feasibility analysis, design/redesign, development, deployment, manage- ment, evaluation, support, training.
3. The dimensions of educational technology include communication/coordination, content/resources, hardware devices and software, implementation, media, and representation formats.
4. Roles of educational technologist include instructional designer, instructional project manager, media specialist, technology coordinator, system administra- tor, developer/programmer, evaluator, and instructor.

# Technology-enhanced Learning

**Introduction**

In this chapter, we argue that a theoretically consistent approach to learning design is to interrelate pedagogical theory with the desired features of learning, and then to map relevant activities and tools along with human and technical resources against learning goals and an appropriate pedagogical approach. This approach is intended to enable educational practice to reflect relevant learning theories. Different learning theories and epistemologies (e.g., behaviorism, cognitivism, constructivism) lead to various conceptions of information processing and knowledge development that influence effective technology use. Given the central functionality of education to help learners acquire and develop declarative, procedural and contextual knowledge, learning theories and technologies are fellow travelers.

The idea of linking learning theories and technologies became important as learning theories become more mature (i.e., cognitivism and social constructivism), and new technologies became affordable and commonplace (e.g., the Internet, social networking). The critical appraisal of the link between learning theories and technologies can be structured around the following observations: (1) changes in society and education have influenced the selection and use of learning theories and technologies; (2) learning theories and technologies are situated in a broad and ill-defined conceptual field; (3) learning theories and technologies are connected and intertwined with information processing and knowledge acquisition and development; (4) educational technologies have shifted in emphasis from program or instructor control toward more shared and learner control; and (5) learning theories and findings represent a complex mixture of principles and applications (Spector, Merrill, van Merriënboer, & Driscoll). In this chapter, the phrases "pedagogical approach" and "instructional strategy" are used interchangeably, although some scholars argue that there are differences in that learning includes non-formal situations as well as structured and formal learning situations.

**Types of Learning Objectives**

1. In the analysis phase of planning instruction, it is reasonable for a designer to consider the kinds of things to be learned (Anderson & Krathwohl). According to Gagné, there are five different kinds of things that can be learned: (a) verbal information (e.g., facts, as in knowing that), (b) cognitive strategies (e.g., selecting a process to address a problem situation, as in knowing why and when), (c) intellectual skills (e.g., using rules to solve a problem, as in knowing how), (d) motor skills (e.g., riding a bicycle, as in performing well.

**Definitions**

**Motor skills:** include physical skills and bodily movements involving muscular activity. Examples of motor skills are drawing a straight line, learning to ride a bicycle, changing a flat tire. Many motor skills also require verbal information, cognitive strategies, and intellectual. As it happens, nearly all of the five types of things to be learned involve some aspects of another learning type, but usually one type of thing be learned is dominant.

**Verbal information:** knowing that something is the case, for example, knowing that there are 24 h in a day or that tides occur twice daily; also known as, declarative knowledge. Examples of verbal information include knowing that insects have six legs or that a byte consists of eight bits (zeros or ones).

**Cognitive strategy:** refers to selecting an appropriate approach to solve a par- ticular problem; a cognitive process that involves awareness of the problem as well as awareness of one's own knowledge and ability relevant to the problem, also known as contextual or causal knowledge. Examples of cognitive strategies include using a split-half approach to solving a troubleshooting problem or applying a bubble sorting algorithm for a selected data set.

**Intellectual skills:** Learning how to do something; also known as procedural knowledge. Subskills include discrimination, concept application, rule using, and problem solving; intellectual skills are also known as procedural knowledge. Examples of intellectual skills include solving equations, sorting objects into cat- egories, and identifying relevant principles to apply in particular situations.

**Attitudes:** internal states which affect an individual's choice of action toward some object, person, or event. Example of attitudes is being predisposed to react in certain ways and having a particular interest in something.

**Discrimination:** Identifying things so as to be able to make different responses to the different members of a particular class. Examples of discrimination tasks include distinguishing different classes of objects, such as flowers, dogs, vegetables, and people of different nationalities.

**Concept application:** identifying and using appropriate concepts (both concrete and abstract concepts). Examples of concrete objects include chairs and tables. Examples of abstract objects include hate and social cohesion.

**Rule using:** applying a rule to a given situation or condition by responding to a class of inputs with a class of actions. An example of rule using is to multiple the probabilities of individual events to determine the probability of both events happening.

**Problem solving:** combining lower level rules to solve challenging problems. Solving problems is the aim of most learning tasks and the tasks are often complicated. The main point is that the type of thing to be learned is an important aspect of instructional planning as it links to learning objectives, activities, outcomes, and assessments. The type of thing to be learned can help one identify a likely instructional method and strategy. There are, of course, other aspects to be taken into account, including the learners, their prior knowledge, and the setting in which learning will take place.

**Instructional Strategies and Types of Learning Objectives**

An instructional strategy is a description of an approach to a particular instructional or learning activity. Instructional strategies are closely linked with the type of thing to be learned. For example, if the thing to be learned is how to remove the radar from an airplane, then it would not be appropriate to only use expository (i.e., telling) or inquisitory (i.e., asking) instruction. This is a procedural task that is best learned by showing and doing—of course, some information is necessary such as where the radar unit is located and what safety precautions must be taken. A strategy for learning such a task could be a combination of demonstrating and modeling the task, and then having learners perform the task, with feedback pro- vided along the way. A variation could be breaking the task down into subtasks and using a part-task approach. For example, the first preparatory steps (e.g., turning off all systems and removing panels to gain access to the radar unit) might be treated as one chunk and practice until mastered. There are many instructional strategies that instructional theorists have developed over the years in addition to the general expository and inquisitory strategies mentioned earlier. Examples include the fol- lowing (these are only meant to be suggestive, as alternative strategies might be appropriate for the instances cited and this list is far from exhaustive):

a. Drill and practice appropriate for learning verbal information that for what- ever reason must be committed to memory.
b. Tutorial instruction appropriate for learning simple procedures or how to navigate within a particular software system.

a. Exploratory instruction appropriate for promoting understanding about phenomena new to the learner.
b. Interactive simulation appropriate for promoting critical reasoning about dynamic, complex systems.
c. Socratic questioning appropriate for helping a learner link something new and seemingly unfamiliar to something already understood.

Lecture appropriate for introducing a new topic and creating some motivation and an appropriate foundation for that topic. Of course, there are many more strategies, and they can be applied in many ways. At a course level, the general approach might be an experiential strategy, but at the unit level a lecture might be effective to introduce basic concepts, and at the activity level, a case-based collaborative discourse or an interactive simulation might be effective. What is important is to align the strategy with the type of thing to be learned. Determining the appropriate strategy for a particular task is an important aspect of instructional design, as already mentioned multiple times. The designer takes into account various strategies suggested by an instructional theory and relevant learning theory, along with the type of thing to be learned and the learners involved, and then describes how to deploy those strategies in order to achieve optimal learning outcomes.

### Mastery Learning

The mastery learning model is based on the assumption that all students of a class can learn and attain the mastery level if sufficient time, adequate instruction, and timely help are provided to them according to their needs, interests, and abilities (Schwartz & Beichner). Therefore, the model focuses on attaining mastery level (i.e., grade A as an indicator of mastery of a subject) by almost all the students, say 95% of a class with due provisions of sufficient time and appropriate types of scaffolding and feedback (i.e., help; see Bloom).

### Programmed Learning

Generally, the learning performed or instruction provided by a teaching machine or programmed textbook is referred to as programmed learning or instruction. Pro- grammed learning is a method or technique of giving or receiving individualized instruction from a variety of sources such as programmed textbook, teaching machine, and computers with or without the help of a teacher (Schwartz & Beichner).

### Simulation

Simulation is used as a technique for providing training to the students. Such type of instructional activities provides powerful learning tools to them (Schwartz & Beichner).Learning theories and technologies are connected and intertwined by information processing and knowledge acquisition. In order to understand the technology-enhanced learning, it is useful to look at the technologies used in different periods of history when the different learning theories emerged and became popularity.

From the 1920s to the 1960s, behaviorism was proposed and came to be dominant. Some technologies were adopted in the process of teaching, such as the automatic teaching machine, chemo-card, etc.In 1924, the psychologist Sidney L. Pressey designed the first teaching machine, which is suitable for rote-and-drill learning. It was mainly used for automated testing of students. It also includes the principle of allowing students to set their own pace, positive response, and timely feedback. The automatic teaching machine includes two modes of operation: quiz and learning. He believes that "teaching machines are unique among instructional aids, in that the student not merely passively listen, watches, or reads but actively responds. In addition, stu- dents could find out whether his response is correct or not, and a record may be kept which aids in improving the materials."In 1930, J. Peterson designed chemo-card which can support automatic scoring and timely feedback.

Cognitivism became dominant in the 1970s and 1980s. Many early educa- tional technology developments occurred in university settings, and these were often associated with various computer technologies, such as PLATO (Programmed Logic for Automated Teaching Operations) and Logo.

PLATO the first generalized computer-assisted instruction system developed in the 1960s at the University of Illinois. It developed many tools to support the design, development, and deployment of learning environments. Many modern concepts in multi-user computing were developed in PLATO, including forums, message boards, online testing, e-mail, chat rooms, picture languages, instant messaging, remote screen sharing, and multi-player games.

In the 1970s, the Logo programming language was introduced to support many instructional activities, and some people thought it would revolutionize teaching and learning in schools. In 1980, Seymour Papert introduced Logo. It was the first language specifically designed to enable children to learn by discovery From the 1980s, constructivism started to become dominant. Interactive multimedia, Internet, and other modern technologies were applied in teaching and learning. In the technology-supported learning environments, learners could con- struct their knowledge actively in interaction with the environment and through the reorganization of their mental structures.

1. With the rapid development of information technology, MOOCs, social networking, cloud computing, etc., are widely used in teaching and learning. The connection between people and people, people and knowledge, knowledge and knowledge changed from ideal to reality. MOOCs are used in distance education which were first introduced in 2006 and emerged as a popular mode of learning in 2012 (Lewin). It is an online course aimed

at unlimited participation and open access via the Web (Kaplan & Haenlein). Learning analytics is the use of intelligent data, learner-produced data, and analysis models to discover infor- mation and social connections for predicting and advising people's learning (Sie- mens).

Information technology has become an important tool of education, and it is not only rich in information resources, but also can extend human capacity and expand the social environment of supporting learning. The history of technology and learning theory's development reflects an evolution from individual toward community learning, from content-driven learning toward process-driven approaches, from isolated media toward integrated use, from presentation media toward inter- active media, from learning settings dependent on place and time toward ubiquitous learning, and from fixed tools toward handheld devices.

In the future, with the development of information technology, learning theories will be improved and developed further. The theories of instructional design will be more mature and more scientific. The practice of educational technology will promote the continuous development of the learning theory and will promote each other.

**Key Points in This Chapter**

1. Learning theories are conceptual frameworks describing how knowledge is absorbed, processed, and retained during learning. In the process of designing and developing instructional systems, learning environments and learning activities relevant to learning theories and psychological perspectives include behaviorism, cognitivism, constructivism, connectivism, and humanism.
2. The major idea of behaviorism includes: (1) The learning process is a gradual attempt and error until the consistent success is attained. (2) The key to learning success depends on reinforcement. (3) Learning involves a stimulus–response sequence.
3. The nine instructional events include: gain attention, inform learners of objec- tives, stimulate recall of prior knowledge, present the content, provide guidance for learning, elicit performance "practice," provide informative feedback, assess performance test, and enhance retention and transfer.
4. Constructivism believes that learning is the process of constructing internal psychological representation in the process of the interaction with the envi- ronment. The constructivism emphasizes learner-centered, situational, collabo- rative, and meaningful construction.
5. The technology and learning theory have interactions. Learning theories and technologies are connected and intertwined by information processing and knowledge acquisition. With the rapid development of information technology, MOOCs, social networking, cloud computing, etc., are widely used in teaching and learning.

**Learning resources**

1. Behaviorism could not explain how children acquire a natural language; also, about the time, mainframe computers were spreading a model of cognitive architecture which was developed with the mind being analogous to a computer processor
2. A timeline figure of learning theories can be added with time on the x-axis from about 1913 (John Watson's "Psychology as the Behaviorist Views it) to 2020 and depth and breadth of coverage on the y-axis—and okay to include behav- iorism, cognitivism, socio-constructivism, organizational learning, and machine learning and perhaps a few other prominent learning theories;

# Skills Of Teaching Methods

**Introduction**

Direct teaching is the pedagogy that makes mastering academic knowledge and skills its central purpose. It can also be used to develop strategies for learning in a wide variety of content areas (Schwartz & Beichner). Behavioral pedagogical approach is appropriate for learning outcomes of motor skills and verbal infor- mation. Possible pedagogical strategies include drill and practice, part-task training,tutorial, games, lecture, and so on. For motor skill learning, possible strategies include hands-on experiences with real and simulated artifacts and interacting with simulations and virtual realities.

**Inductive Thinking**

The inductive thinking model is an example of concept formation based on allowing students to infer a general rule or patterns based on multiple examples and non-examples; this approach was developed. Learning how to classify is fundamental; consequently, students learn information and concepts through the activity of classifying. They also learn how to build conceptual understanding of content areas and how to build and test hypotheses based on classifications. Inductive thinking is a generic model, partly because classification is believed to be the basic higher-order thinking skill and further, because the model is applicable to knowledge from phonics to physics.

**Concept Attainment**

The concept attainment model facilitates the type of learning referred to as con- ceptual learning in contrast with the rote learning of factual information or of vocabulary. In practice, the model works as an inductive model designed to teach concept through the use of examples. Therefore, in addition to help the students in the attainment of a particular concept, the model enables them to become aware of the process of conceptualizing.

**Advance Organizers**

As Ausubel maintains, advance organizers are the primary means of enriching or strengthening the learner's cognitive structure and enhancing the possibilities of learning or retention of new knowledge or information. Ausubel describes advance organizers as introductory materials or activities presented ahead of the learning task and at a higher level of abstraction and inclusiveness than the learning task itself. Their purpose is to explain, integrate and interrelate the material in the learning task with the previously learned material (Ausubel). Advance organizers increase the ability to absorb information and organize it, especially when learning from lectures and readings. Possible uses include learning cognitive strategies and intellectual skills (e.g., discrimination tasks, learning concepts, engaging in exploratory learning and simulations). Socratic questioning can be a form of an advance organizer. Possible technologies are management flight simu- lators, interactive simulations, and puzzles (Suchman's), an inquiry training system, or intelligent tutoring system, among others.

**Group Investigation**

Group investigation is a pedagogical approach that allows a class to work actively and collaboratively in small groups and enables students to take an active role in determining their own learning goals and processes. Examples for group investi- gation are observing the behavior of insects in groups, discovering the motion curve of an asteroid within a scientific team (Sharan & Sharan). Small group investigations are often used in problem-based medical training.

**Classroom Meeting Strategy**

The classroom meeting model is a multipurpose approach for classroom manage- ment by setting aside time for students to discuss classroom issues as a group. Examples of a classroom meeting model are holding class meetings to involve students in addressing question like "How should cheating be handled?" or "What can we do about teasing and bullying in our school?" (Class Meetings— TeacherVision, n.d.). While classroom instruction has been much criticized, it has a wide range of applicability.

**Project-Based Learning Approach**

Project-based learning is a pedagogical approach that encourages active learning within the constraints set by the teacher. Within this framework, students pursue solutions to non-trivial problems by asking and refining questions, debating ideas, making predictions, designing plans and/or experiments, collecting and analyzing data, drawing conclusions, communicating their ideas and findings to others, asking new questions, and creating artifacts. With the support of today's technology, project-based learning is making a strong comeback in the classroom. Throughout the process, students use digital tools for gathering information and multimedia to create learning artifacts. They are guided by what they think the end result of their project should be. The teacher coaches the team to keep students on task and keep their work productive while students develop self-management and collaboration skills. By providing peer feedback on the content and demonstrating respect for their own findings, more substantive content is learned. The end product of each team is often presented to the whole class, demonstrating their understanding of what they learned.

### Inquiry Based Learning Approach

Inquiry-based learning approach is a method with which students learn knowledge driven by specific questions or a complex problem. The teacher scaffolds and helps students as they make contributions, identify questions, and gather relevant data on the Web. The setting of the problem is crucial during this process.

Collaborative inquiry holds process similarities with project-based learning although it is distinctive in its focus on a driving question, or a complex problem, with respect to which students gather data for later analysis. In inquiry-based learning, the setting of the problem is as important as, if not more important than, finding solutions. The teacher scaffolds and helps students as they make contri- butions, identify questions, and gather relevant data on the Web. With mobile technologies, data from the field become more easily accessible with analytic tools to make sense of what has been gathered.

Possible technologies to support the constructivist approach include toolkits and other support systems. Access to resources and expertise offers the potential to develop engaging, student-centered, active and authentic learning environments; Microworlds and simulations are likely technologies.

### Collaborative Learning

Collaborative learning is broadly defined as a situation in which two or more people attempt to learn together (Dillenbourg) or to accomplish shared goals (Johnson & Johnson). Characteristics of effective collaborative learning include positive interdependence among members, group and individual account- ability, interpersonal skills, the ability to self-monitor, ensure consistent progress, and discontinue patterns of behavior that impede the progress (Johnson & Johnson). Collaborative learning is a situation in which two or more people learn or attempt to learn something together. Examples for collaborative learning are parents completing a task with their kids, participating in community economic activities (Collaborative Learning). Small groups of 3 to 5 learners are often effective, and on occasion, roles may rotate among the members of a group to ensure that everyone learns all aspects of the task (Johnson & Johnson).

### Collaborative Knowledge Building

Collaborative knowledge building focuses on problems and depth of understanding; it takes steps of the creation, testing, and improvement of conceptual artifacts in groups. Knowledge building represents an attempt to refashion education in a fundamental way, so that it becomes a coherent effort to initiate students into a knowledge creating culture. Accordingly, it involves students not only developing knowledge building competencies but also students coming to see themselves and their work as part of the civilization-wide effort to advance knowledge frontiers. In this context, the Internet becomes more than a desktop library and a rapid mail delivery system. It becomes the first realistic means for students to connect with civilizationwide knowledge building and to make their classroom work a part of it (Sardamalia & Bereiter). Examples of knowledge building are group discussions, interactive questioning, dialogue, and so on.

### Types of Technology for Educational Uses Technology

According to Rogers, a technology is a design for instrumental action that reduces the uncertainty in the cause-effect relationships involved in achieving a desired outcome. Others define a technology as a systematic application of knowledge to solve a problem valued by a group or society. In both cases, the aim of a technology is to achieve a desired outcome.

A technology may have two components: (1) a hardware aspect, consisting of the tool that embodies the technology as a material or physical object, and (2) a software aspect, consisting of the information base for the tool. Some technologies lack one or both of these components and may simply consist of a standard pro- cedure or general purpose algorithmic approach.

### Educational Technology

Educational technology is not a homogeneous intervention but refers to a broad variety of modalities, tools, and strategies for learning. Its effectiveness, therefore, depends on how well it helps teachers and students achieve the desired instructional goals (Bruce & Levin).

Bruce & Levin describe a new way of classifying uses of educational technologies, based on a four-part division suggested years ago by John Dewey: inquiry, communication, construction, and expression. Each of these is briefly described next.

### Technologies for Inquiry

What follows are lists of technologies, tools, and techniques likely to be appropriate to support inquiry.

- Theory building technology as media for thinking
- Model exploration and simulation toolkits
- Visualization software
- Virtual reality environments
- Data modeling-defining categories, relations, representations
- Procedural models
- Mathematical models
- Knowledge representation and integration tools such as semantic networks, and outline tools
- Data access connecting to the world of texts, video, data
- Hypertext and hypermedia environments
- Library resources
- Digital libraries
- Databases
- Repositories with music, voice, images, graphics, video, data tables, graphs, text, etc.
- Data collection using technologies to provide enriched input
- Remote scientific instruments accessible via networks
- Microcomputer-based laboratories, with sensors for temperature, motion, heart rate, etc.
- Survey makers for student-run surveys and interviews
- Video and sound recordings
- Data analysis methods and technologies
- Exploratory data analysis
- Statistical analysis
- Environments for inquiry
- Image processing
- Spreadsheets
- Programs to make tables and graphs
- Problem-solving programs.

### Technologies for Communication

- Document preparation
- Word processing
- Outlining
- Graphics

- Spelling, grammar, usage, and style aids
- Symbolic expressions
- Desktop publishing
- Presentation graphics
- Communication with others
- Electronic mail
- Asynchronous computer conferencing
- Synchronous computer conferencing (text, audio, video, etc.)
- Distributed information servers like the World Wide Web
- Student-created hypertext environments
- Collaborative media
- Collaborative data environments
- Group decision support systems
- Shared document preparation
- Social spreadsheets
- Teaching media
- Tutoring systems
- Instructional simulations
- Drill and practice systems

### Technologies for Construction and Problem Solving

- Lego components, tangram puzzles, Rubik's cube
- Computer-assisted design software
- 3D printing.

### Technologies for Knowledge Representation

- Sensors and using technologies such as QR Codes, GPS displays
- Graphs and charts
- Drawing and painting programs
- Music making and accompaniment
- Music composing and editing
- Interactive video and hypermedia
- Animation software
- Multimedia composition.

### Principles for the Selection of Technology for Educational Uses

Mayer has proposed some principles of multimedia learning which can also be used for guiding the selection of technology for educational uses. The principles are as follows:

1. **Principle of Appropriateness**

   - Technology should promote the general and specific goals of the class.
   - Technology should be appropriate to the intended level, including vocab- ulary level, difficulty of concepts, methods of development, interest appeal.
   - Technology should be either basic or supplementary to the curriculum.

2. Principle of Authenticity

- ○ Technology should present accurate, up to date, and dependable information.

3. Principle of Cost

- ○ Substitutes and trade-offs of alternative solutions should be considered.

4. Principle of Interest

- ○ Technology should catch the interest of the learners, must stimulate curiosity, or satisfy the learner's need to know.
- ○ Technology should have the power to motivate, encourage creativity, and imaginative response among users.

1. Principle of Organization and Balance

- ○ Technology should be well organized and well balanced in content.
- ○ Purpose of the material should be clearly stated or perceived.
- ○ There should be logical organization, clarity, and accordance with the principles of learning such as reinforcement, transfer, and application in the materials.

**Key Points in This Chapter**

1. The kinds of instructional strategies that should be selected depend on learning objectives and learning domains; the technologies should be aligned with instructional strategies.
2. In order to achieve the learning objectives, learners engage in learning activities, such as inquiry, communication, construction, and knowledge representation. Types of learning and pedagogies should be considered when selecting appropriate technologies.
3. Pedagogical approaches relevant to the selection of technologies include practice and feedback approaches, representational approaches, collaboration approaches, project-based approaches, inquiry-based approaches, and informal and autonomous learning approaches.
4. The principles for the selection of technology educational uses include the principle of appropriateness, the principle of authenticity, the principle of cost, the principle of interest, and the principle of organization and balance.

# Principles Of Teaching

**Introduction**

People learn what they do; this principle is derived from behavioral psychology (e.g., reinforcing a desired behavior makes it more likely to recur) and finds support in neural science (e.g., when an action is repeated often, the neural connections in the brain associated with that action are strengthened, making it more likely to recur in the future an implication of this basic principle is that learning activities should be designed with desired future performance in mind.

These principles are integrated throughout this book and will hopefully become second nature to you as an educational technologist. In addition, it is well estab- lished that prior learning is generally predictive of future learning—that is to say, that learners who have struggled with a subject in the past are likely to continue to struggle. This implies that being aware of a learner's prior experiences and per- formance can help an instructor develop appropriate learning activities for that learner. Moreover, technology can play a key role in helping an instructor develop personalized and individually appropriate learning activities, as will be discussed in a later chapter.

**Defining Educational Technology**

The term "educational technology" is widely used within the education profession as well as in the general population. It might seem like there is no need for a definition of such a commonly used term. However, such an assumption might be made for the everyday use of the term "philosophy" and many other terms that identify areas of scholarly pursuit. As it happens in most of those cases, the various professional and scholarly communities have provided a specific definition of the term as a way to clarify the aims and scope of the discipline. In this case, we begin with the definition provided by the Association for Educational Communications and Technology "the study and ethical practice of facilitating learning and improving performance by creating, using and managing appropriate technological processes and resources".

In elaboration of the AECT definition, we note that designing, adapting, cus- tomizing, implementing, testing, deploying, and evaluating resources, activities, and learning and instructional tools intended to facilitate learning, performance, and instruction are included within the scope of the discipline. In addition, we emphasize the notion of *practice* in the definition for two reasons. First, it is directly aligned with the basic Greek derivation of the first term, *techné*, involving the notion of skill. Second, throughout this volume there will be an emphasis on the *effective use* of a technology to support or facilitate learning, performance, and instruction. That notion aligns particularly with the second term, *logos*, involving the notion of reason. In ordinary terms, one might then say that educational tech- nology involves the reasoned and effective use of technology to support or facilitate learning, performance, and instruction.

**For the instructor**: Ask, for examples, of educational technologies and then ask how an example satisfies or fits the definition above.The popular use of "technology" is in reference to physical things or things that one can touch, see, hear, taste, or smell.

In computer science, the term "technology" often refers to both hardware and software, both of which can in principle be perceived one way or another. The AECT definition is not restricted to physical things or things that are perceivable as it refers to both processes and resources. Both will be discussed in this volume, consistent with the AECT definition. In many cases, however, we will use a separate term to refer to a process or collection of processes, such as *instructional design* or a *pedagogical approach* or a learning strategy all of which can be considered specific kinds of processes, with examples such as problem-based learning or flipping the classroom or hands-on training.

While many will associate *learning* and *instruction* with education, some might wonder why the definition includes *performance*. Definitions of "learning" and "instruction" are needed to make the inclusion of performance obvious. Learning is characterized by stable and persisting changes in what a person or group of people believe, know, and are able. Intentional learning is purposeful and goal-driven, which is common in formal learning situations. Instruction is comprised of those things and processes that are intended to support, facilitate, or enhance learning—intentional learning in this context.

The performance of learners is used to establish that a stable and persisting change has occurred, which is one reason to include performance within the pur- view of educational technology. It is an effective use of a technology that matters, and improving what learners know and can do is an indication of an effective use. Moreover, because an instruction consists of all those things aimed at improving learning, including those involved in designing and supporting learning, their performance is also relevant to the discipline. A well-designed device or artifact used poorly or improperly by a teacher is not likely to support learning. Teacher performance and, as a consequence, teacher preparation and professional development in technology use are important. Likewise, a poorly designed learning environment may contain a wealth of information and resources, but a poor design can easily inhibit an effective use. As a consequence, the performance of instructional designers is also relevant to educational technology. Moreover, there is a discipline called "performance tech- nology" associated with human resource management.

Associated with the notion of performance in the context of effectiveness is the notion of efficiency, which can be linked to productivity. Both effectiveness and efficiency can be applied to learners, teachers, and designers also to administrators, support personnel, and policy makers. Later in this volume, a great deal of emphasis will be placed on effective learning and things that are likely to contribute to effectiveness, such as learner motivation, engagement, empowerment, and timely and meaningful formative feedback.

**For the learner:** Start an educational technology journal or diary on paper or in digital format, and entitle a first entry "a memorable learning experience that I consider effective, efficient, and engaging." Identify things in or about that experience that are likely linked to its effectiveness.

### A Brief History of Educational Technology

Learning is a natural ongoing process that occurs in organized situations as well as in everyday activities. As such, the history of learning is coincident with the history of human beings. Teaching also has a long history that is roughly coincident with the history of human families and tribes. Various tools and techniques have been used to support teaching and learning throughout the ages, so one can also conclude that educational technology has a very long history. It is common to divide human history into broad periods or epochs such as the primitive period, the agricultural period, the industrial period, the information age, and the emerging era of the intelligent society (see the last chapter in this volume for more on this emerging era.

Early in human history, it is likely that actual objects were used to support learning. For example, an elder teaching a young child to hunt might use an actual spear to support helping the child learn to aim and throw, perhaps initially at a tree rather than at an animal. The abacus was an early calculating device used to keep track of inventories, and its use had to be trained as responsibility shifted from one person to another.

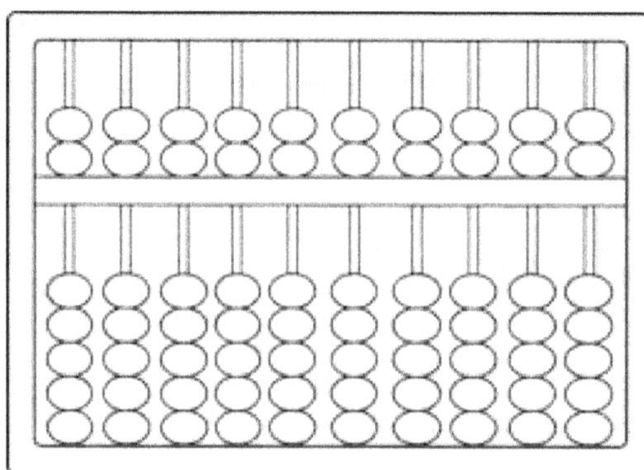

Fig 1.1 The abacus

**For the learner:** Compare the abacus (see Fig. 1.1) and the slide rule with regard to functionality and periods in which they were introduced. Reflect on their use and how others were trained to make use of them. What is especially noticeably different about using an abacus to make a calculation and using the slide rule to make the same calculation?

From very early times, records were kept and histories were recorded on scrolls and in pictographs that were used to teach each new generation things that had transpired and that might affect their futures. People learned trades on-the-job using actual tools for many years; apprenticeship and on-the-job training remain in use in many fields.

The invention of the Gutenberg printing press in the fifteenth century made it possible to share information and knowledge with a much wider group of indi- viduals than had previously been the case. Its use had become widespread in Europe by the sixteenth century, and books became a primary resource used in many educational settings. It is worth noting that it took a hundred years or so for the printing press technology to be widely adopted. How long did it take smartphones to become widely adopted? The printing press transformed learning and instruction as well as social, political, and economic arrangements, although it took a couple of hundred of years for those transformations to occur. Are similar transformative effects likely to occur on account of new and emerging technologies?

For the instructor: Conduct an in-class or group discussion of the rate of adopting a new technology in terms of planning for a new technology and then its introduction into a context to the time it takes to make an effective use of that technology.

In the nineteenth century, non-text media arrived with the invention of the daguerreotype (early camera) in 1839 and wireless transmission of electromagnetic waves (early radio) and the kinetoscope (moving pictures) in the 1890s. The twentieth century is when technologies to support learning, per- formance, and instruction rapidly increased, with television and animations in the first half of the century and computers and the Internet in the second half of the century.

What can be concluded based on this brief history? It is obvious that tech- nologies change. Technologies are changing at an ever-increasing rate. Will this rapid rate of change continue? If so, what are the implications for educational technology in the remainder of the twenty-first century?

Technologies change what people do. Many have said that the printing press changed education. Prior to the introduction of printed books, education was limited to small groups of specially selected people, and training was conducted in a one-to-one or a one-to-a-few setting, typically in the workplace or in the presence of a teacher/ mentor. Books brought information to the masses and made it possible to have larger groups involved in education and to supplement training with materials that could be studied outside the workplace. Formal learning became more stan- dardized as well as more available. From Plato's Academy established in Athens circa 387 BCE with a small number of students to the Martin Luther University of Halle-Wittenburg established in 1502, there was a change from a small group of students following one teacher's oral teaching to a public institution with students following multiple teachers and using standard texts.

Technologies change what people can do. As new technologies emerged, it became possible to represent information and knowledge in many forms, including pictures, graphics, animations, and movies. Multiple modes of representation have emerged. In addition, multiple forms of communication have also emerged. In addition to one-to-one and one-to-many face-to-face communication modalities, there are multiple forms of digital communication, including Internet chat rooms, videoconferencing, discussion forums, social networks, and more.

For the learner: Make and date an entry in your educational technology journal entitled "Leading Educational Technologies in Use Today." Then, make a second entry entitled "Anticipated Educational Technologies of the Future".

Technologies also change what people want to do. As more and more resources became available, especially at the end of the twentieth century, many people began pursuing areas of personal interest, and there has been a steady growth in informal learning as a consequence. Many students now want to experience things in school that are relevant to the kinds of jobs and careers they plan to pursue. Students who have smartphones and use them outside school want to be able to use them in school as well, often to the dismay of teachers and possible disruption of intentional learning activities.

In keeping with the principle that people learn what they do, David Merrill has described instructional things that are likely to promote desired learning outcomes. Merrill argues that instruction should be centered on meaningful and realistic problems, which was probably the case for those being trained to use an abacus or slide rule. In addition, the instruction can be described in terms of four kinds of things: telling, asking, showing, and doing.

**For the instructor:** Conduct an in-class or group discussion relating Merrill's first principles of instruction to Gagné's nine events of instruction ples and Gagné's events are evident in this chapter?

In general, there has been a shift in emphasis in formal learning situations to include more *showing* and *doing* and somewhat less *telling* as a result of the powerful technologies now available. While it seems like the best of times in terms of what can be done to use technologies to effectively and efficiently support learning, performance, and instruction, it may seem like the worst of times for those who are charged with designing, maintaining, and sustaining the technologies used to support learning. Instructional designers have many more options in choosing resources and support mechanisms than ever before. Establishing what works best with whom and in various situations is more difficult than ever before. Cost models are dynamic, in part because technologies are now rapidly replaced by newer technologies. Training teachers to make effective technologies that change so rapidly is an ongoing challenge.

For the learner: Recall the activity to describe making a calculation with the abacus and the same calculation with the slide rule. What difference did you note? Someone might argue that to make an effective use of the slide rule, one first needed to have an expectation about the range for a reasonable solution since it is very easy to misalign the cursor line on the slide rule and make a big mistake as a result. The act of reflecting in advance on the problem and a reasonable answer might be considered a learning activity or a form of asking oneself. Make an entry in your educational technology journal on the learning value of reflecting and instructional value of asking as a means to encourage reflection. Provide an example based on your own experience.

Edsger Dijkstra in argued that computers had yet to solve a single problem; they had only introduced the new problem of learning to use them effectively. That claim seems especially applicable to educational technology in light of the history and the recent explosion of new technologies. The reason for including a brief history of educational technology is not to highlight how far the discipline has come. Rather, it is to remind those entering the discipline and contributing to its continued growth and success that:

- It is seldom the case that there is one right solution or approach to a learning problem or situation involving educational technology, especially given the rich variety of situations and technologies.
- What worked for Plato in his academy may not work well in a twenty-first-century school; it is clear that what people call the Socratic method and then praise did not work out that well for Socrates (Plato's teacher) given how the citizens of ancient Athens reacted for those not familiar with Socrates, he was jailed and executed due to his peripatetic teaching; the city leaders accused Socrates of corrupting the youth.
- Planning for the effective and efficient use of educational technologies involves planning for the future replacement of a particular technology and the resources, processes, and pedagogical approaches associated with that technology.
- Planning for the future is especially challenging given the rate of change in available technologies; however, educational technologists should plan for the future and subsequent chapters in this volume will suggest new technologies that are emerging and what their impact might be (spoiler alert:smart learning environments and personalized learning may be coming soon to a theater near you).

# Perspectives Of Educational Technology Systems Perspective Of Educational Technology

**Introduction to Systems**

Austrian biologist Ludwig Von Bertalanffy (1901–1972) is known as one of the founders of general system theory that was published in 1968. According to Ber- talanffy, a system is defined as a set of elements standing in interrelation among themselves and within an environment (Bertalanffy). Peter Michael Senge (born 1947) is an American system scientist and the founder of the Society for Organizational Learning. Senge is known as the author of the book *The Fifth Discipline: The Art and Practice of the Learning Organization*, which focuses on group problem solving using the system-thinking methods in order to convert companies into learning organizations.

Systems are pervasive in the natural world (e.g., the solar system, the nervous system, various ecological systems, etc.) as well as in things created by people (e.g., a governmental system, a school system, a library system, etc.). In short, we live in and interact with systems every day in many different ways. The focus of this chapter is on systems involving education and technology, of which there are many and likely to be many more in the future.

A system is a combination of more than two interacting and interconnected elements which function as an organic or integrated or coordinated whole. There are three main aspects of a system.

1. A system consists of two or more elements. Systems are pervasive. Many objects and processes involve systems.
2. A system is more than a collection of elements and includes how the elements are connected and how they interact over time. Systems change over time. Change and development of each system occurs in the exchange of material, energy, and information, which can benefit the dynamic stability and openness of these systems simultaneously.

A system is a kind of bounded whole that is situated in a particular envi- ronment or context, with input coming from the environment and outputs going back to the environment. Systems exist in an environment. Each system accompanied by its surrounding can generate a larger/broader system, and those parts contained in the original system can be regarded as the subsystem of the new one.

**Elements of a System**

A system can be described in terms of five basic element: (1) the various components comprising a system. (2) interactions among the components of a system; (3) the environment in which the system exists; (4) inputs from the environment to the system; (5) outputs from the system to the environment (Mangal & Mangal).

In general system theory, a system is any collection of interrelated parts that together constitute a larger whole. These component parts or elements of the system are intimately linked with one another, either directly or indirectly, and any change in one or more elements may affect the overall performance of the system, either beneficially or adversely.

**Solar system and the human body system are the typical examples of a system.**

1. The solar system is made up of the sun and eight planets (Mercury, Venus, Earth, Mars, Jupiter, Saturn, Uranus, and Neptune) along with smaller planetary objects; the solar system includes the mutual interactions among these elements (e.g., gravitational influence), their orbits, as well as influences from the milky way galaxy which is the environment in which the solar system exists.
2. The human body is comprised of several systems, including the nervous system, the skeletal system, the endocrine system, the exocrine system, the blood circulatory system, the respiratory system, the digestive system, the urinary system, and the reproductive system.
3. These systems coordinate with each other to carry out their different physiological functions.
4. The human body exists in an environment

**Education Systems** :Roger Kaufman (1972) was one of the first to apply a systems approach to edu- cation. An education system is a man-made system and can be considered as a subsystem of the society in which it exists. One might think of an education system as taking inputs from the society (e.g., students) and providing outputs to society (e.g., graduates). Moreover, an education system could be conceptualized as a collection of subsystems, such as a school system, a curricular system, a grading system, and so on.

**Elements of an Education System**

According to the characteristics of the system, the education system can be cate- gorized to different levels: (1) macro-level: state, social education system;

(2) meso-level: community and school education system; (3) micro-level: teaching process, learning process, media development, and other education system. The school system may be treated as a subsystem of the education system or a system complete in itself (Mangal & Manga). In this chapter, we mainly focus on the school education system at the meso-level, and the structure of the education system.

An education system includes four kinds of elements:

(1) inputs: pupils, administration, teachers, material for formal or informal education;

(2) processes: formal or informal education process;

(3) outputs: people who have attained educational objectives, such as grades and abilities;

(4) and an environment: formal learning venues (e.g., schools) and informal learning venues (e.g., home, café, etc.).

In addition, the system consists of interactions among these elements.An instructional system is a subsystem within an education system, although one can describe elements and interactions relevant to an instructional system (e.g., resources, assessments, instructors, students, scaffolding, etc.).

One can also consider a curriculum as a subsystem within the larger instructional system. In short, one can elaborate an education system in terms of subsystems.All the system analysis of current system teaching methods.

**Principles for an Education System**

## 1.  Overall principle

A system should be effective in fulfilling its purpose. An instructional system should have integrity, in the sense of being reliably effective; this is the essential characteristic of a system and the core of system theory. A system is composed of elements within an environment and should interact in a way that fulfills the purpose of the system. The overall principle of an education system requires coordinating the relationships among teachers, learners, and resources.

**2.Feedback principle**

A system should be stable. From a system dynamics point of view, there are two kinds of feedback mechanisms within a system—positive or reinforcing feedback and negative or balancing feedback. As an example, the moon is orbiting the earth at a speed of more than 3600 km an hour. At that speed, it would keep going into outer space and not return each day; in this case, one can say that gravitational attraction of the earth on the moon serves as a balancing mechanism or a kind of negative feedback control that keeps the system stable and the moon in orbit around the earth.

The feedback principle tells us that an instructional system also has feedback mechanisms. One can think of assessments as a kind of balancing mechanism that helps to keep an instructional system stable. If all students simply attended and then left without any kind of assessment (neither formative nor summative), the system would become unstable and unable to attain its intended purpose of helping stu- dents develop knowledge and master skills. If all that matter in an instructional system are the number of participants without any consideration of learning, then the system is unlikely to fulfill its instructional purpose. Some have criticized early massive open online courses (MOOCs) for this very reason.

3.  **Order principle:** Order refers to the nature and structural functions of a system. Systems can be categorized

along a simple-to-complex scale. Systems can also be categorized along a disordered-to-ordered scale. Given the prior mention of thinking about an edu- cation system as a collection of subsystems, one can then categorize the subsystems as progressing along these two scales (simple-to-complex, and disordered- to-ordered).

Typically, an education system will have complex but ordered subsystems. One might argue that if one thinks in terms of grade-level educational subsystems, they do progress from simple and relatively disordered at an elementary level to a more complex and more ordered level as one proceeds to a secondary and tertiary level.

**Educational Technology from a System's Perspective**

Educational technology is an area that uses systematic methods to analyze educa- tional problems, design and develop instructional systems to support learning. A system's perspective views the various elements and interactions in a systemic manner, functioning in a well-ordered manner just as a healthy human body with its various subsystems functioning in a well-ordered manner. In addition to that sys- temic perspective, instructional designers and educational technologists typically employ systematic methods and processes to ensure that stable instructional systems result. This systemic view and the associated systematic methods and processes have evolved over time, as indicated in the brief overview of recent educational tech- nology history for a more comprehensive treatment).

**Five Stages of Educational Technology**

Educational technologies have evolved from simple texts to highly complex and interactive digital systems. depicts a simplified view of that development. The important point here is that education systems have become very complex, which results in the increasing challenges in designing, developing, implementing, and supporting these systems.

Typical Educational Technology Systems with the use of technology in education system, the educational technology sys- tems are changing rapidly. The typical educational technology systems developed

**Intelligent Computer-Assisted Instruction**

In the traditional CAI, the computer is only used as the disseminator of knowledge, but it does not understand the knowledge that it teaches; moreover, it does not understand the students beyond a simple parsing of text-based responses. With the development and maturation of artificial intelligence, AI technology is used in more sophisticated CAI system so that the CAI system can understand what to teach, how to teach, and how a student is progressing, which leads to the emergence of the intelligent computer-assisted instruction (ICAI). ICAI is a kind of application mode of CAI, which is based on artificial intelligence, cognitive science, and thinking sciences. ICAI constructs a simple cognitive model of learners using established characteristics and processes of human thinking. Through an ICAI system, students can acquire knowledge through individualized adaptive learning.

ICAI changes the traditional teaching mode. The students get feedback infor- mation in real time through human computer interaction, adjusting the learning pace actively. The whole teaching process is shifted from teacher-centered to student-centered. In 1970, the first influential ICAI system was the scholar system that taught South American geography, creating a precedent for ICAI research.

An ICAI system has a computer program that uses artificial intelligence tech- niques (e.g., a production model, backward chaining, and other means) for repre- senting knowledge and performing an interaction with a student to stimulate and control his learning in a given field. In an intelligent instructional system, the student is actively engaged with the educational environment and his interests and misunderstandings drive the tutorial dialogue (Bottino & Molfino).

It must be pointed out, however, that from an educational point of view, ICAI systems are not only expert systems, but they must also embody suitable models both for the student's behavior and for the teaching methodology (Bottino & Molfino).

**Intelligent Tutoring System**

The innovative feature of ICAI was to support individualized learning for students. Intelligent tutoring system (ITS) is a typical instance of an ICAI system. ICAI and ITS are often used interchangeably.

An ITS is a computer system that aims to provide immediate and customized instruction or feedback to learners (Psotka, Massey, & Mutter), usually without requiring intervention from a human teacher. It can assist students in studying a variety of subjects by posing questions, parsing responses, and offering customized instruction and feedback. During the rapid expansion of the web boom, new computer-aided instruction paradigms, such as e-learning and distributed learning, provided an excellent platform for ITS ideas.

The ITS is the typical educational technology system, including four technology components: (1) domain model, (2) learner model, (3) pedagogical model, and interaction model. Presents a typical ITS architecture.

**Domain Model**

The term "domain" means a specific field or scope of knowledge, such as algebra, critical thinking, and psychology. People who have a deep understanding of a domain are called *domain experts*. A domain model represents domain experts' ideas, skills, and the way that they solve domain problems. A good domain model provides a structure to minimize domain experts' authoring time and maximize the quality of the content (Robert).

The domain model contains the set of skills, knowledge, and strategies of the topic being tutored. It normally contains the ideal expert knowledge and also the bugs, mal-rules, and misconceptions that students periodically exhibit (Robert). The domain model consists of the concepts, facts, rules, and problem- solving strategies of the domain in context. It serves as a source of expert knowledge, a standard for evaluation of the student's performance and diagnosis of errors (Ahuja & Sille).

**Learner Model**

We simply need to record, represent, and track characteristics of the learner before, during, and after learning. The practical problem is that it is expensive to identify, track, store, update, and later retrieve the ever-growing universal set of variables.

**The Typical Example of ITS**

AutoTutor is an intelligent tutoring system developed by researchers at the Institute for Intelligent Systems at the University of Memphis in 1997. The goal was to help students learn physics, computer literacy, and critical thinking using an intelligent tutorial (Graesser, Chipman, Haynes, & Olney).

AutoTutor is a computer tutor that helps students learn by holding a conversation in natural language (AutoTutor). It has produced learning gains across multiple domains (e.g., computer literacy, physics, critical thinking). Three main research areas of AutoTutor are: human-inspired tutoring strategies, pedagogical agents, and technology that supports natural language tutoring.

**Key Points in This Chapter**

1. A system is defined as a set of elements standing in interrelation among themselves and within an environment.
2. A system can be described in terms of five basic elements: the various com- ponents comprising a system; interactions among the components of a system; the environment in which the system exists; inputs from the environment to the system; outputs from the system to the environment.
3. An education system includes four elements of inputs, process, output, and environment.
4. The educational technology has gone through five stages: intuitive instruction, visual instruction, audiovisual instruction, audiovisual communication, and information and communication technologies.
5. The typical educational technology systems include CAI, ICAI, and ITS.

# Educational Technology Systems

**Introduction**

The previous chapter discussed a systems' perspective of educational technology. Educational technology can be regarded as a system with a variety of components and relationships. As we know, educational technology systems aim at improving user's performance, and users could include students, teachers, parents, support personnel, administrators, and policy makers. Different users may have different perspectives and concerns, and thus user's perspectives play a vital role for the success of educational technology systems.

In software engineering, user-centered design and development are now standard practice with an emphasis on rapid prototyping and getting input from represen- tative users. Taking the typical models of user-centered design in software engi- neering as a reference and considering the research of user-centered design in educational technology, the following sections will introduce the users' perspective of educational technology. Emphasis is on user experience, user-centered design, learner-centered design, and the ARCS motivation model.

### Definition

User experience (UX) is defined as "a person's perceptions and responses that result from the use or anticipated use of a product, system or service". From to this definition, UX includes all the users' attitudes, emotions, perceptions, preferences, physical/psychological responses, and behaviors that occur *before, during, and after use*. The ISO also lists *three factors* that influence user experience: system, user, and the context of use.

### User Experience Honeycomb

Morville created a frequently reproduced honeycomb model to design for user experience that illustrated the facets of user experience, especially to help clients understand why they must move beyond usability.The user experience honeycomb could be used as a guide to explain the various facets of the design of user experience. Morville believed that the user experience honeycomb would contribute to educating clients, which helps them to find a sweet spot between the various areas of a good user experience. If applied in educational technology, the essential items could be explained as follow:

**Useful.** An educational technology product or service should fulfill teachers'/ students'/parents' needs. If the product or service could not fulfill user's wants or needs, then there is no real use for the product itself. Usable. Systems in which the product or service is delivered should be simple, familiar, easy to understand and easy to use. The learning curve that users must go through should be as short and painless as possible.

**Desirable.** The visual aesthetics of the educational product, service, or system should be minimal, attractive, and easy to understand. Our pursuit of efficiency must be moderated by an appreciation for the power and value of the brand, image, identity, and other elements of emotional design.

**Findable.** Information in the educational technology systems needs to be findable and easy to navigate. If teachers/students/parents have a problem, they should be able to find a solution quickly. The navigational structure must be set up in a way that takes users' behaviors and habits into consideration to makes sense.

**Accessible.** The product or services should be designed so that even users with disabilities can have the same user experience as others.

**Credible.** The enterprises and their products or services need to be trustworthy. Valuable. Our products or services should deliver value to sponsors. For nonprofits, the user experience must improve the mission of the enterprise. With for-profits, it should contribute to the bottom line and increase customer satisfaction.

Take a Web site design as an example. The content should be original and fulfill some users' needs (useful). The site must be easy to use (usable). The design elements (like the brand) are used to evoke emotion and appreciation (desirable). The content needs to be navigable (findable), and they should be available even to people with disabilities (accessible). Users must trust the content and the brand (credible).

The honeycomb model helps to find all the areas that are essential to a good user experience and can be broken down into more specific aspects. As an educational technology sysy system/product designer, we could use the honeycomb model to outline and define all the areas that are relevant to user experience (UX) design, and ask ourselves the following questions. Is it more important for our system to be find- able? Is it desirable to use? Which of those two concerns need to be addressed first? Do we need to improve credibility in our market? Is our product or service accessible? So on and so forth.

### User-Centered Design Definition

The term "user-centered design (UCD)" was used in the 1980s in Donald Norman's research laboratory at the University of California San Diego and became widely used after the publication of the book entitled: *User-Centered System Design: New Perspectives on Human-Computer Interaction* (Norman & Draper).

Landauer defined UCD as "design driven, informed, and shaped by empirical evaluation of usefulness and usability". Later, Karat defined UCD as "an iterative process whose goal is the development of usable system... achieve through the involvement of potential users of a system in system design. It captures a commitment that you must involve users in system design" .From the two definitions, we see that UCD is a broad term to refer to the design processes in which users influence how a design takes shape.

### User-Centered Design Process

UCD is both a broad philosophy and a series of methods. Lots of techniques could be used to involve users in UCD, but the important concept is that end users should be involved one way or another in the design process. For instance, users may be consulted about their needs and be involved at different stages during the design process, such as the requirements gathering process or the usability testing process. In some types of UCD methods, users may have a deep impact on the system/product design by being involved throughout the design process.

**In the process of planning UCD, the following four activities is the key to success.**

1. Understand and specify the context of use: Identify who will use our product, what is the purpose of using it, and in which conditions they will use it.
2. Specify the user and organizational requirements: Identify any business mis- sions or end-user needs that must be met for our product to become successful.
3. Produce design solutions: This step should be a spiraling process, building from a rough concept to a complete design.
4. Evaluate designs against user requirements: The evaluation to see if our product meet user's needs—usually through usability testing with actual users—is as important as quality testing to good software development.

### User-Centered Design Principles

In the above iterative process of UCD from ISO 13407, the following six principles should be considered by UCD managers.The design should be based on clear understanding of environments, users, and tasks.

1. Users should be involved throughout the design and development process.
2. The design should be driven user-centered evaluation and then refined by user-centered evaluation.
3. The design process should be iterative.
4. The design should address all the areas of user experience.
5. The design team should include multi-disciplinary skills and perspectives.

**Norman proposed the following *seven guiding principles of design* to ensure useful and usable products.**

1. Use both knowledge in the world and knowledge in the head. Build con- ceptual models based on research and investigation, write manuals before the design is implemented, and make sure the manuals are easily understood.
2. Simplify the structure of tasks. Understand that users can only remember five things at a time on average and therefore not to overload their short-term memory. It is important to provide mental aids for easy retrieval of information from long-term memory. Make sure the user has control over the tasks, and the tasks should be consistent.
3. Make things visible to facilitate execution and evaluation. The user should be able to figure out the use of an object

by seeing the right buttons or devices for executing an operation.

4. Make the connection of operations obvious. One way to make connections of functions understandable is to use graphics.

5. Exploit the power of constraints. These can be both natural and artificial, and their use gives the user the feeling that there is one thing to do.

6. Design for error. Plan for errors to be made by users; one way to do this is to provide allowed the option of quick and easy recovery from any possible error made.

7. When all else fails, standardize. Create an international standard if something cannot be designed without arbitrary mappings.

Norman's work stressed the need to fully investigate the desires and needs of the end users and the possible uses of the product. Users became a central part of the product development process. Their involvement will contribute to more effective, efficient, and safer products and lead to the acceptance and success of our products.

**Involve Users in the Design**

In order to involve users in the design, the first and most important task is to identify who is the user. Eason proposed three kinds of users: primary, secondary, and tertiary users. *Primary users* are those who actually use the product; *secondary users* are those who will occasionally use the product or those who use it through a mediator; *tertiary users* are those who will be affected by the utilization of the product or make decisions about its purchase. The successful design of a product must consider the wide range of stakeholders/users of the product. Not everyone who is a stakeholder needs to be represented in a design team, but the effect of the product on them must be taken into consideration.

After the stakeholders have been identified, a thorough investigation of their needs should be conducted by doing tasks and needs analyses. Then, designers can develop alternative design solutions to be evaluated by the actual users. In both the design process and evaluation process, users should be involved in. Ways to involve users in the design, development.

**Learner-Centered Design**

Comparing with UCD, learner-centered design (LCD) emphasizes the importance of supporting students' growth and their motivational needs in designing educa- tional software. Learner-centered indicates a move from ease-of-use issues toward the development of a student's comprehension and expertise the difference between users and learners.

- Users have the expertise in their work domains, and they understand the tasks they are accomplishing. Learners do not have the same domain knowledge as the user. They have neither the expertise of the work area nor the understanding of specific tasks of a professional counterpart.

- Users are homogeneous. They are engaged in specific work activities and share the same work culture, so they can be considered homogenous in some meaningful ways. Learners are heterogeneous. They may not share a common culture, background, or understanding, so designers must consider the differences in the background, the diversity of learning styles, and other kinds of varieties of the learners' groups.

- Users, by the nature of involvement in their work tasks, often have intrinsic motivations for their work, and tools do not have to provide any additional motivational incentives. However, learners' intrinsic motivations may differ from those of experts. Besides, because learners lack understanding of the work area, they may face more obstacles in completing the task at hand, thereby reducing their motivation even more.

- Users do not necessarily need to learn about their work from the tools. Instead,they need tools to help them finish their work. However, learners should learn when they engage in a new field of work by using educational software. So their tools, just as the learners themselves, (i.e., their windows in the field of work) need to grow and change.

User-centered design should address the conceptual distance between computer users and the computer. However,the learner-centered design should focus on the gulf of expertise that lies between novice learner and an expert in the knowledge domain.So, if we putting learners at the center of the product design, the special needs of learners must be considered:

- Understanding is the Goal. When design the educational software, keep in mind that learners do not have the basic knowledge and skill in specific work domains. For example, they will not know the accounting principles or practices when a spreadsheet is presented to them. How will they learn to use that spreadsheet must be considered in the design process?
- Motivation is the Basis. We cannot count on the motivation of learners. Remember that both students and professionals have a strong tendency to fritter away time or to procrastinate, when they are confronted with a task that they are not familiar or unprepared for. The educational software should be designed to support the learner's wavering motivation.
- Diversity is the Norm. Learners who use the specific tool are often from a diverse set of backgrounds, with various interests, skills, abilities, learning styles, etc. "One size fits all" will not satisfy the various needs of diverse learners.
- Growth is the Challenge. Learners can be very different from day 1 to day 100. They may have learned quite a bit about a problem domain and might have developed a set of skills and practices in that domain; however, most of the software doesn't change and grow. The individual has changed, but the knowledge and the specific practices of a task in the software haven't.

**Therefore, learner-centered design must follow *these basic tenets:***

- Take learner's understanding as the result (through coaching, modeling, and critiquing).
- Create and maintain learner's motivation (through low cognitive load and immediate success feedback).
- Offer a wide range of learning techniques (by using different media and different ways of expression).
- Encourage the learner's growth (through an adaptable product). In other words, good scaffolding should be designed for students, and the scaffolding is available when the student needs it, but not when they want to study inde- pendently. Motivation can also be sustained by putting learners in the context of doing, developing software that enables them to construct artifacts and com- municate with others about those artifacts.

Another theory should be mentioned for designing learning experience, the universal design for learning (UDL), which is a framework to improve and optimize teaching and learning for all people based on scientific insights into how humans learn. Recognizing that the way individuals learn can be unique, the UDL frame- work drew upon from neuroscience and education research, was first defined by David H. Rose in the 1990s. UDL is a framework for developing lesson plans and assessments based on the following three main prin- ciples (Meyer, Rose, and Gordon):

**Provide multiple means of engagement (the "why" of learning):** UDL encourages teachers to look for multiple ways to motivate students. Letting kids make choices and giving them assignments that feel relevant to their lives are some examples of how teachers can sustain students' interest. Other common strategies include making skill building feel like a game and creating opportu- nities for students to get up and move around the classroom.

**Provide multiple means of representation (the "what" of learning):** UDL recommends offering information in more than one format. For example,textbooks are primarily visual. But providing text, audio, video, and hands-on learning gives all kids a chance to access the material in whichever way is best suited to their learning strengths.

**Provide multiple means of action and expression (the "how" of learning):**UDL suggests giving kids more than one way to interact with the material and to show what they've learned. For example, students might get to choose between taking a pencil-and-paper test, giving an oral presentation, and doing a group project.

**The ARCS Model of Motivational Design**

- The ARCS model of motivational design is a theory created by John Keller rooted in analyzing the motivational characteristics of learners. It is a problem-solving approach to design the motivational aspects of learning environments to promote and sustain students' motivation to learn.According to the ARCS model, there are four interrelated phases for stimulating and sustaining learner's motivation in the teaching and learning process: Attention, Relevance, Confidence, Satisfaction (ARCS).

### Attention

- Attention in this theory refers to the interest of students in learning the concepts/ideas being taught. According to Keller, there are two general ways to stimulate students' attention. (1) Perceptual arousal uses surprise or uncertainly to gain interest and uses novel, surprising, incongruous,and uncertain events; (2) Inquiry arousal stimulates curiosity by posing challenging questions or problems to be solved.

  In details, designers or teachers could use the following six methods to gain the students' attention.

  **Active participation:** using strategies to get learners involved in the learning material/subject matter, such as games, role play or other hands-on methods.

  **Variability:** using a wide range of methods in presenting material to enhance presentation and account for diversity in learning styles, such as videos, short lectures, mini-discussion groups.

  **Humor:** using a small amount of humor to motivate attention (but not too much to be distracting).

  **Incongruity and conflict:** using statements that go against learners' past experiences to provoke conflict and incongruity.

  **Specific examples:** using a visual stimulus, story, or biography.

  **Inquiry:** posing questions or problems for the learners to solve, such as brainstorming activities.

  **Relevance:**According to Keller, relevance could be established to increase a learner's motivation, by using language and examples that the learners are familiar with. The following six major strategies could be used to establish relevance.

**Experience.** Tell the learners how the new learning will use their existing skills. We best learn by building upon our preset knowledge or skills.

- Present worth. What will the subject matter do for me today?
- Future usefulness. What will the subject matter do for me tomorrow?
- Needs matching. Take advantage of the dynamics of achievement, risk taking, power, and affiliation.
- Modeling. First of all, "be what you want them to do!" Other strategies include guest speakers, videos, and having the learners who finish their work first to serve as tutors.
- Choice. Allow the learners to use different methods to pursue their work or allowing a choice in how they organize it.

### Confidence

- Confidence in the ARCS model focuses on building positive expectations for achieving success among learners. Learner's confidence level is often asso- ciated with motivation and the amount of effort that they put in completing a performance objective In order to increase confidence, the following strategies could be considered. Help learners understand their likelihood for success. If they feel the objectives could never be accomplished or that the cost (effort or time) is too high, their motivation will shrink.
- Provide objectives and prerequisites. Help learners evaluate the probability of success through clarifying performance requirements and assess- ment criteria. Guarantee that the students are aware of performance requirements and assessment criteria.

- Allow for success that is meaningful.
- Grow the learners. Allow small steps of growing during the whole learning process.
- Feedback. Provide feedback and support internal attributions for success.
- Learner control. Students should feel some degree of control over their learning and assessment. They should believe that their success is a direct result of the amount of effort they have put forth on their learning.

### Satisfaction

- Learners must be rewarded or satisfied in some way, whether it is the praise from a higher up, a sense of achievement, or mere entertainment.

  The following three main strategies could be used to promote satisfaction.

Intrinsic reinforcement. Encourage and support intrinsic enjoyment of the learning experience. The teacher invites former students to provide testimonials on how learning these skills helped them with sub- sequent homework and class projects.

- Extrinsic rewards. Provide positive reinforcement and motivational feedback. Example: The teacher awards certificates to students as they master the complete set of skills.

- Equity. Maintain consistent standards and consequences for success.

Example: After the term project has been completed, the teacher provides evaluative feedback using the criteria described in class.

### Key Points in This Chapter

- UX is a person's perceptions and responses that result from the use or antici- pated use of a product, system, or service; system, user, and the context of use are the three factors that influence UX.
- The honeycomb model to design for UX includes the seven elements of useful, usable, desirable, findable, accessible, credible, and valuable.
- **Meaning:** UCD is a broad term to describe design processes in which end users influence how a design takes shape. Understand and specify the context of use, specify the user and organizational requirements, produce design solutions, and evaluate designs against user requirements are the four key activities for the success of UCD.
- **The principles of UCD include:** The design is based upon an explicit under- standing of users, tasks, and environments, Users are involved throughout design and development, the design is driven and refined by user-centered evaluation, and the process is iterative. The design addresses the whole user experience; the design team includes multidisciplinary skills and perspectives.
- **There are three types of users:** Primary, secondary, and tertiary. The differences of users and learners include their knowledge in the task domain, the homogenous population or diverse population, their motivation to engage in the task, the change of knowledge and skills, and the design focus.
- **The key strategies for LCD include:** Understanding is the goal, motivation is the basis, diversity is the norm, and growth is the challenge.
- **There are four steps for promoting and sustaining motivation in the learning process:** Attention, Relevance, Confidence, Satisfaction (ARCS) in the ARCS model for motivational design.

# Experience And Learner Experience

**Introduction**

Every day, people go to school, participate in classes and school activities, and have learning experiences. The idea that students have learning experiences seems simple enough, but what is meant by a learning experience?

We all know that a singular experience is made up of an infinite amount of minor experiences, relating to contexts, people, and products. Moreover, the experience can be divided into different stages. Please think of your experience of camping on a huge mountain, which might be made up of smaller experiences, such as seeing the trees, rivers, feeling the breeze, and you recognize it appreciated and the climb from the bottom to the ascent, during the process you have interactions with products such as one's tent and cook stove, and interactions with companions on the trip. Moreover, when you come back from the camping, you tell the story of climbing the mountain to your peers, which you may refer it as "a terrific experience."

Often, the word "experience" and the concept of "user experience" are used during product design and development processes. We want initially to create a systemic way to talk about the experience broadly. Our understanding of existing theories of experience has led to three ways that we speak of experience: cognitive experience, an experience, and experience as a story.

**Definition of Experience**

The purest form of reference is experience, the constant stream that happens during moments of consciousness. Self-talk or self-narration is often the way that people acknowledge the passing of this kind of experience (Forlizzi & Ford). This definition is based on cognitive scientist Richard Carlson's theory of consciousness known as Experienced Cognition (Carlson). The above example mentioned that "one sees the beautiful landscapes, and feel pleasant" is an example of such experience.

Another way to talk about experience is to talk about having an experience— what philosopher John Dewey referred to in his book Art as Experience (Dewey). This type of experience has a beginning and an end, and changes the user, and sometimes, the context of the experience as a result. For example, your experience of climbing the mountain. Another example of an experience is wit- nessing a story that allows us to feel powerful emotions, assess our system of values, and possibly make changes in our behavior. The University of Pennsylvania Oncolink has a powerful selection of stories written by those who have experienced cancer themselves, or through loved ones, leading us through an experience as we read them.

A third way to discuss experience is to talk about experience as a story, an idea that has been discussed at length. Stories are the vehicles that we use to condense and remember experiences and to communicate them in a variety of situations to certain audiences. Experience as the story plays an important role in events as diverse as legal testimony and fantasy gaming. Because experience as the story is naturally communicative, it has relevance for sharing user findings with a design team of various disciplines.

At present, the definition of user experience given by ISO is widely recognized. According to the ISO. 9241-210 standard, "user experience is the cognition and response generated from the use of a product, system or service and expected use" (ISO FDIS 9241-210).

The definition of the learning experience is close to the user experience in that both involve cognitive processing and subsequent responses. Learning experiences represent the user experience from a learner's specific perspective in the interaction with an educational product or learning environment (Huang, Hu, & Yang).

**Learning Experience**

Learning experience is a notion derived from user experience and is also a general kind of experience that may have associated feelings and biases. The subject of a learning experience is the learner, just as the subject of a user experience is the user. Learning experiences can be understood as a variety of experiences through the learning process, and in the learning environment.

According to the previous discussion, learning experiences can be defined as learners' perceptions, responses, and performances through interaction with a learning environment, educational products, resources, and so on.

Information processing learning theory can be used to explain such a process (Anderson, Matessa, & Lebiere, Likewise, Gagné pointed out that the learner perceives various things and, after a series of information processes, the learner forms a conceptualization and then reacts (Gagné).

Learners' perception of learning environment mainly refers to their perception of the people and the things, including resources, tools, learning community, com- munity education, learning styles, and teaching methods (Huang, Yang, & Hu). Perception enables a person to carry out actions in an environment (Elnaga). According to Mahlke's user experience model, learner perceptions can deepen cognitive processes and impact emotions and feelings.

Perceptions can lead to follow-up actions, attitudes, and emotional experiences. A response to a learning experience can include emotional reactions and other kinds of responses. Performance in a learning experience mainly refers to the learner's behavior, including associated constructs such as learning effectiveness, efficiency, and achievement. Learning effectiveness refers to the degree to which intended out- comes were attained; learning efficiency refers to the time and effort to attain those outcomes; learning achievement not only emphasizes the achieving intended out- comes, but includes satisfaction and other related subjective experiences, such as confidence and continued interest in the subject area.

As devices, products, software, systems, and services are increasingly included in learning, it is important to view learner experience in a holistic manner that includes all aspects of experiences. For example, in a healthy classroom learning environment, the students, teachers, and designers will be turning to concepts of sustainable design to address comfort-related issues such as hygiene, safety, acoustics, and availability of space, natural daylight and natural ventilation. For a technology-rich classroom, the learning technology in a classroom encompasses virtual technologies, such as online presence and online resources, installed appliances, such as media presentation systems, remote interaction sys- tems, and room-scale peripherals, and mobile devices. So the learner experience in a classroom includes the experience of the learner in using furniture, equipment, devices, software systems, and services.

**Elements of Learner Experience with Educational Technology**

Educational technologies can be divided into the following four categories: learning tools, educational resources, learning environments, and learning methods.

1. Learning tools are those digital and non-digital media used for the purpose to facilitate learning through interactions between people and systems, such as learning applications, multimedia devices ("learning tools," 2017). Examples of learning tools include flash cards, mind maps, blogs, electronic dictionaries, expert systems, Web 2.0 tools, electronic performance support systems (EPSSs), mobile educational apps, table computers, and so on.Learning resources are materials that can be used to support teaching, learning and research, such as textbooks, course readings, and other learning content.

**MOOC**

Learning resources include educational video clips, open educational resources, massive open online courses (MOOCs), and online libraries and repositories.

1. Learning environments refer to the diverse locations, contexts, and cultures in which students learn, such as classroom, cyberspace (Learning Environment). Learning environments include traditional classrooms as well as online learning management systems.
2. Method is "a way, technique, or process of or for doing something". (Definition of Method, n.d.) Learning method stands for the way of presentation of the specific contents of a subject that may be properly grasped and understood by learners.
3. Drill and practice, memorization, inquiry-based learning, collaborative learning, competency-based learning.
4. System Analysis of Education system works all learning works.

**Principles for Meaningful Learner Experience with Educational Technology**

Learner experience with educational technology includes learners' perceptions, responses, and performances of the learning environment, resources, and methods. The structure and elements of user experience can reveal the connotation and extension for the definition, which could enlighten us the structure and elements of learner experience with educational technology. Morville proposed a con- ceptual framework called user experience honeycomb to describe the elements of user experience in designing Web sites.

**In order to create a meaningful and valuable user experience, the information in a Web site should be:**

1. Useful: the content should be original and fulfill a need;
2. Usable: the Web site should be easy to use;
3. Desirable: image, identity, brand, and other design elements should evoke desirable emotion and appreciation;
4. Findable: the content should be navigable and locatable onsite and offsite;
5. Accessible: the content should be accessible to people with disabilities;
6. Credible: users should trust and believe what they see, hear, or read; and
7. Valuable: the Web site should deliver something valued by the user.

Rubinoff also proposed that user experience was made up of four inter- dependent elements: branding, usability, functionality, and content. Branding includes all the aesthetic- and design-related items within a Web site. Branding refers to the site's projection of the desired organizational image and message. Functionality includes all the technical and behind-the-scenes processes and applications. It entails the site's delivery of interactive services to all end users, and it is important to note that this sometimes means the public as well as adminis- trators, instructors, and learners. Usability entails the general ease of use of all site components and features. Subtopics beneath the usability banner can include navigation and accessibility. Content refers to the actual content of the site (text, multimedia, images) as well as its structure, or information architecture. We look to see how the information and content are structured regarding defined user needs and client business requirements.

To help define the objectives and scope of user experience efforts, as well as enable their meaningful measurement, Guo suggested a conceptual frame- work that describes four distinct elements of user experience, including value, usability, desirability, and adoptability, and how they interact with one another in driving better product designs.

Learner experience in a learning environment with educational technology needs to consider classroom as an integrated system with classroom furniture, equipment and devices, software systems, and services. The four elements of user experience for products can be used to express the learner experience with educational tech- nology. While learner experience should consider the diversity of learners in a learning environment, we use "adaptability" to replace "adoptability" to show the diversity of needs from students. Also, the physical environment factors, such as light, temperature, and acoustics, play a major role for experience. So "comforta- bility" is also included in learner experience. Through the above analysis, the elements of learner experience include value, usability, desirability, adaptability, and comfortability.value is the core element for learner experience with educational technology, which focuses on whether an educational product meets the needs of learners and whether it is effective for learning. Usability deals with the issue whether it is easy to use an educational product, services, resources, device, etc. Adaptability focuses on the flexibility of an educational technology and deals with the issue whether it adapts to learners' different needs. Desirability asks for whether an educational technology is fun and engaging for learners; and com- fortability focuses on whether learners feel comfortable with the technology.

Based on the above-proposed element, in the following section, technology-rich classroom would be illustrated as an example to show what indicators should be used to evaluate whether an educational technology is suited for learning

**Indicators to Evaluate Learner Experience**

Learner experience with educational technology could be designed, improved, and assessed by considering the five elements of learner experience. Value is the most core indicator of learner experience, and the other four elements should support and contribute to value. Services, equipping, and furnishing are the main factors in a technology-rich classroom, of which the indicators of learner experience derived from depicts a technology-rich classroom at Beijing Normal University called a smart classroom, because it can adapt to the learner's needs. The learners in the picture are freshman majoring in educational technology. Learners are using their smart phones to scan the QR Code shown on the screen to get access to course resources Value

**Do Learners Value the Technology** : From the holistic perspective, the value of learner experience refers to the positive or negative quality that renders the changes of the classroom, such as classroom furnishings and layout changes, the use of equipment, desirable or valuable for the learners.

What drives an educational technology's value to the student? Educational technology features must be in alignment with learning needs. If a classroom change is designed to support learning needs, teacher and learners may consider the layout changes and equipment valuable. Learning needs encompass more than just their explicit needs things that learner know they want, but to include learners' implicit needs things that learners do not express as needs, which might be hidden in learning activities and be recognized by their teacher. To meet learners' unexpressed needs, educational technology should not only be easy-to-use products, such as devices and software, but also services that add much value to student learning.

Usability Do the Learners Find the Technology Easy to Use?

Usability refers to the ease of use and learnability of educational technology, which is composed of:

1. Learnability: how easy is it for teachers and students to accomplish basic tasks the first time they encounter the educational technology?
2. Efficiency: once teachers and students have learned the design of educational technology, how quickly can they perform teaching and learning tasks?
3. Memorability: when teachers and students return to the design after a period of not using it, how easily can they establish proficiency?
4. Errors: how many errors do teachers and students make, how severe are these errors, and how easily can they recover from the errors?
5. Satisfaction: does the educational technology meet the needs of learners?

The design factors of an educational technology include systems, facilities, and software which have a significant influence on usability. Operating systems provide a software platform for the application programs to run. Microsoft Windows, Mac OS X, GNU/Linux are examples of popular operating systems being used in personal computers. Operating systems, with diverse features, provide different software to support various resources and learning activities. The facilities include devices, audio–video control system, projector, interactive whiteboard, student response system, and access to the wireless network.

Software systems include learning management systems, resources providing system, and collaborative learning platform. Classroom network tools offer new possibilities for classroom interaction; they present ways of rapidly distributing information, exchanging ideas, and constructing shared artifacts that can support a variety of engaging and mathematically rich activities that would be more difficult or even impossible to implement in conventional classrooms. Within the context of learning tasks, a large part of desirability is attributable to innovative and recognizable design in user interface and interaction. User interface design includes well-organized navigation, nice-looking graphics, and sleek designs. Meanwhile, important, a desirable educational technology must engage the learner in their purpose of using.

Based on the above analysis, the following indicators for evaluating the usability of technology-rich classroom are proposed: (1) Is it easy to switch to another operating system? (2) How difficult is it to update the software and hardware involved? (3) Is it easy to access the Internet? (4) Are data connections available for different types of devices, such as USB, VGA, HDMI, etc.? (5) Are the user interfaces friendly and intuitive?

**Desirability—Do Learners Enjoy Engaging with the Technology?**

Desirability refers to the attractiveness and engagement of the activities in educa- tional technology or the pleasing perception from teachers and students. A perva- sive goal in education is to engage students in learning so that they are attentive and mindful (Lavigne & Mouza).

**Engagement involves three dimensions (Fredricks):**

a. behavior (e.g., participation in activities such as the number of times students interact with virtual world characters, embedded tools, objects),
b. cognitive-motivational (e.g., putting forth the effort, the belief of competence in the content area or self-efficacy, desire to be optimally challenged),
c. emotions (e.g., interest, curiosity, sense of belonging, and affect). Engagement in an educational technology depends on the content presentation methods, the digital resource, software systems, and interactive design.
d. Vahey et al. listed four key benefits when using dynamic-representation technologies in mathematics classrooms: (a) providing rich representations for the student to understand some difficult concepts, (b) providing an opportunity for the student to focus their attention on the same point, (c) supporting the utilization of narrative as a type of representation, and (d) engaging students in the class. Dynamic-representational environments have also been shown to increase student engagement in mathematics.
e. In order to promote young children's collaborative communication and thinking skills in science learning activities, Kershner et al. suggested that the interactive white board can be used collaboratively in a variety of science activities closely related to common classroom practice, for that whiteboards provide the opportunity for children to interact with learning content, and it can satisfy the needs of more desirable vivid interaction for children.

### Adaptability—Do Learners Find the Technology Personally Adaptive?

Adaptability of an educational technology deals with the diversity of students and their learning preferences which result in a need to treat learners as individually as possible. Room layout should be flexible to meet the teacher's instruction and learner's collaboration; a software system should adapt to learning styles of the learners; and physical environment factors, such as lighting, temperature, and ventilation, should be adjusted to suit learners.

Hill recognized that flexible, modern learning environments have potential to encourage students to participate in activities with peers as they acquire knowledge for themselves. About classroom layout, Lippman in studies of schools mentions that providing a variety of spaces within a single classroom may support child–adult/ student–teacher interactions. Jamieson recognized that formal spaces such as lecture theaters, classrooms, and laboratories should have flexible layouts which support a diversity of teaching and learning approaches, although this is not always affordable or feasible.

From the above analysis, combined with the emerging technologies and the main furnishing elements, we propose these questions for evaluating the adaptability of technology-rich classroom

(1) Does the software system provide instant feedback?
(2) Can students present and share their learning outcome easily?
(3) Are the systems compatible with common devices?
(4) Do data between the student and teacher change easily?
(5) Is the classroom layout flexible for different learning activities?
(6) Can the lighting system adapt to learners needs and available daylight?

### Comfortability—Do Learners Feel Conformable with Educational Technology?

Comfortability with educational technology focuses on providing physical and emotional well-being experience to learners when they are using educational technology, i.e., the user interface and environmental conditions consisting of various elements such as temperature, humidity, noise, thermal, air pressure, ven- tilation, air quality, acoustic, dust, vibration, lighting, airflows, radiation, and so on. Due to the increased use of media and technology in classrooms, the design of easy-to-use, adjustable lighting systems is more critical than ever. Lighting needs to be designed to the standards proposed by Illuminating Engineering Societies and the National Electrical Code's current recommendations. Lighting should be designed to meet the special program requirements for each instructional spaceb Also, some studies show that the following factors are important design considerations:

1. Indoor air quality—mold and airborne bacteria have adverse effects on chil- dren's and teachers' health.
2. Temperature and humidity—creates conditions which lead to Sick Building Syndrome, related absenteeism, and lowered mental acuity.
3. Ventilation and airflow—is an occupational health and safety issue because children require more air than adults. Studies indicate that airflow from win- dows is inadequate in schools to remove or prevent the buildup of carbon dioxide. Poor airflow leads to poor performance of tasks.
4. Thermal comfort—there is an optimum temperature for learning, retention, task performance, and job satisfaction.
5. Acoustics—good acoustics (quality rather than the amount of noise) are fun- damental to academic performance.
6. Building age, quality, and aesthetics—affect student and teacher perceptions of safety and well-being. Building age is not as important as the quality of con- struction conditions. Students perform better in modernized or new environ- ments, but it is hard isolating mediating factors, and therefore inconclusive.
7. Furniture, carpets, dampness, and pollutants can lead to health problems such as asthma.
8. Based on the critical factors for comfortability, the following indicators for evaluating the comfortability in a technology-rich classroom are proposed:

    1. Does the lighting system support reading healthy? (2) Does air in the classroom meet the air quality standard? (3) Is the temperature in the classroom suitable for learning? (4) Does the classroom have good acoustics? (5) Does classroom decoration meet the students' preference? (6) Is the learning device easy to operate?

**Key Points in This Chapter**

1. With the fusion of technology, pedagogy, and space, learner experience with an educational technology gradually became essential for ensuring students' engagement and performance.
2. Learning experiences can be understood as learners' perceptions, responses, and performances through interaction with the learning environment, educa- tional product, resources, and so on.
3. Value, usability, adaptability, desirability, and comfortability are the five ele- ments in educational technology that will influence learner experience, which should be considered when build or rebuild learning space.
4. Learner experience will change when the furnishing (providing an audiovisual system, computers, devices, and software) and equipping (decorating classroom and changing layout) in educational technology changed, and service was one of the most key factors for improving learner experience with educational technology.

# Social Learning

**Introduction**

Social media is changing communication between individuals and organizations. People can now enjoy a new type of learning by integrating social media. With the aid of the Internet, learners can get access to courses, instructional materials, and co-learners anytime and anywhere. In addition, learning with social media can provide a high degree of interactivity among participants who are separated both geographically, temporally, and culturally. Social media afford students many of the benefits of face-to-face interaction without the need to travel to specific places at specific times.

In this chapter, we will introduce educational technology from the perspective of social learning and discuss the roles of technology in social learning, describe ways to build and manage learning community, and indicate methods to measure group learning.

### Definition

Social learning was proposed who believed people learn from others through observation, imitation, and modeling. For example, when a child sees one is punished for stealing, the child knows stealing is bad behavior. However, Bandura's definition does not emphasize the social context that is often important for learning describes social learning as active social participation in a com- munity of practice. Wenger and others stress the dynamic interaction between people and the context as they construct meanings and develop identities. In a sense, this is an extension beyond behaviorism and cognitivism to take into account the influence of others and the context analyze social learning in terms of individual understanding, a community of practice, and social interactions in that community as follows:

Social learning may be defined as a change in understanding that goes beyond the indi- vidual to become situated within wider social units or communities of practice through social interactions between actors within social networks .

### Benefits of Social Learning

Social learning emphasizes the fact that individuals learn from social interactions in communities and groups. When students act as a part of a group, they can gain experience during collaboration and develop the important skills of critical think- ing, self-reflection, and co-construction of knowledge.Specific benefits of social learning can be summarized into four major categories: social, psychological, academic, and assessment as follows:

### Social benefits:

- *Contributes to the development of social support system for students.* Learners work in groups or communities through social learning, so they could get suggestions and information from others to deal with questions and problems.
- *Helps to build various understanding among learners and instructors.*
- Thedifferent experience of learner would result in various understanding to same things. Positive relationships between different kinds of people are encouraged in social learning to develop broad perspective and understanding.
- *Establishes a positive atmosphere for collaboration.* Learners participate in peer interactions usually hold a positive attitude and motivation that lead to active social responses to problems and results in a friendly environment.

### Psychological benefits:

- *Student-centered instruction increases students' self-esteem.* In a social learning setting, instruction is learner-centered; learners are responsible for conducting inquiries, applying knowledge, and making meaning of new concepts.
- *Cooperation reduces anxiety.* In social learning setting, learners are usually in supportive environments to manage

conflict resolution and get help to solve problems.

- *Develops students' positive attitudes toward teachers.* In a social learning setting, the environment is open, which allows a teacher to have smooth conver- sations with students. In addition, teachers can better know students and give proper guidance.

### Academic benefits:

- *Classroom results are improved.* Compared with face-to-face teaching, students in social learning deliver more complete reports, make higher quality decisions, and perform better on complex tasks that require groups to generate ideas and solutions.
- *Critical thinking skills are promoted.* When a learner interacts with others, the learner can analyze information from a broader perspective, which could improve his/her critical thinking skills.
- *Students are actively involved in the learning process.* The learner is the center in a social learning context, so learners own the responsibility for learning. They are actively involved in the learning process and more likely to be interested in learning.
- *Problem-solving techniques are enhanced.* When students work in pairs or small groups, one person is listening, while others discuss the question under inves- tigation. All involved are developing valuable problem-solving skills by for- mulating and discussing ideas while receiving immediate feedback from co-learners.

### Assessment benefits:

- *Collaborative teaching techniques utilize a variety of assessments.* In social learning settings, the instructor has more chances to interact with students. Thus, instructors can assess students based on the quality of interactions in addition to exams and other artifacts.

### Features of Technology in Social Learning

Nowadays, technology plays a vital role in social interactions. Example technolo- gies include Facebook, Friendster, LinkedIn, MySpace, Ning, Twitter, and WeChat. These tools involve large-scale networks and the ability to interact in and contribute to large groups. Blogs and wikis are also used but lack many of the benefits of social media tools.

Social media is beneficial in promoting social learning, such as providing community platforms, learning resources and contents, and learning activities. Resta & Laferrière summarize the features of technology in social learning as follows:

***To promote student collaboration and knowledge creation.***Collaboration can be thought of as the process of shared creation. With the interactive nature of technology, students can communicate with others conveniently and represent knowledge clearly, which results in students' active and deep engagement in collaboration.

***To enhance student cognitive performance or foster deep understanding.***Social interaction is considered as a source of cognitive advancement. With the help of technology, students could get smooth communication with each other. For example, mind management tools and concept maps can help present ideas clearly to support reflective thinking and deep understanding.

***To add flexibility of time and space for social learning.*** The virtual workspace has been increasing its popularity in people's daily life. Students can finish their work in different place and time; thus, they can overcome the trouble of place and time. For example, in MOOCs, although students come from different countries, they can work together because of virtual space provided by the course

***To promote student engagement and keep track of student collaboration.***Learning analytics and big data are useful in monitoring learner progress. Many learning platforms can track and analyze the behavior and learning processes to monitor and predict student's achievements and recommend interventions to pro- mote learning.

### Social Learning and Computer-Supported Collaborative Learning

There is an obvious relationship between social and collaborative learning as suggested. In addition, when technology is added to the mix, the relationship of computer-supported collaborative learning (CSCL) and social learning is worth highlighting. Key aspects of CSCL build on Vygotsky's social development theory and incorporate Stahl's collaboration to suggest a pedagogical approach that emphasizes he shared construc- tion of knowledge and understanding.

**Building and Managing Learning Communities and Groups**

**The Five Stages of Group Development**

Before building a group, how a group develops should be understood. Effective group development follows a structured process.Tuckman and Jensen summarized that process regarding five stages: forming, storming, norming, performing, and adjourning.

*Forming:* People with same goals come together, and they need to know the similarities and differences of the team members. The critical thing at this stage is to let members becoming familiar with each other and their task. Discussing the scope of the effort, formulating the methods to deal with the task, and establishing the rules of engagement are relevant at this stage.

*Storming:*When the group attempts to accomplish a task, conflicts about responsibility, division, or rules may surface. The important things at this stage are listening to others, clarifying ideas, finding solutions, and testing ideas.

*Norming:* When the group overcomes a conflict, the members become more actively engaged and more involved in sharing information, maintaining commu- nity, and solving new issues. The important thing at this stage is group awareness that the group is effective. Indicators of group effectiveness at this stage are the clarification of interaction processes and taking actions to address problems.

*Performing:*When the group reaches this stage, members are genuinely inter- dependent, and the group has developed a real unity. Group members are highly oriented to tasks; they collaborate smoothly and play different roles according to the group needs. The important thing at this stage is solving problems in the best way to promote group development. Not all group can reach this stage.

*Adjourning:* The group is not always active or developing. A group can be terminated when the task is over or when the group disbands for any reason. The important thing at this stage is concluding the achievement, recognizing member's contributions, and giving members the chance to say good-byes to each other.

Group development is not always linear. The group process can loop back to storming when there are unsolved conflicts, or when new members join or diffi- culties in understanding tasks arise. Establishing rules of engagement in early stages of a group development will help when the group encounters problems in later stages.

**Building and Managing Small Groups**

In a classroom environment, grouping has multiple possibilities. The person who will decide the grouping (students, teachers, or randomly assigned), depends on the task setting and group characteristics. Before considering the grouping, the group size should be determined. The ideal size of the group depends on the purpose and content of classroom teaching, but it is generally considered that four to five people are optimal. Several issues should be considered in determining the number of groups :

- *How long does it take for a group to learn?*
- *How much experience have the students had?*
- *How old are the students?*
- *What materials are available for students to use?*
- *How comprehensive are these materials?*

After the group size is determined, different methods can be applied. Dreyer and Harder proposed four methods to build groups in classroom settings.

- *Randomly*
- *According to scores*

- *According to interest*
- *According to feelings.*

When students are grouped, there is often a situation where someone is not included; the teacher needs to persuade the group to accept those students not already included in the group. Therefore, the task of grouping is often done by the teacher. Whichever grouping method used, students should be given a chance to change to another group. If students have the opportunity to participate in the selection of partners, their acceptance of learning with their partners will also increase. Thus, the freedom to change partners will play a positive role in pro- moting student participation.

After the team has been identified, the role of each team member in accom- plishing the task needs to be clarified. Through this clear division of labor, the team can work together to enhance their confidence. In addition, the role of team members can vary depending on the task.

**Building and Managing Communities**

Learning communities provide necessary support for social learning. Learners interact with others in learning community and group to form social relationships. However, the establishment and management of a learning community need time and effort and follow the group development law. Essential elements for estab- lishing prosperous learning communities are informality, familiarity, honesty, openness, heart, passion, dialogue, rapport, empathy, trust, authenticity, disclosure, humor, and diverse opinions. According to the five stages to build a projected course, we propose the four stages of building and managing learning community:

1. ***Introductions:***This step is a getting-to-know-you phase. Some methods, such as self-introduction and ice-breaking tasks, can be used to create an initial and emotional connection with others in the community.
2. ***Involved within the group:***his step is a deeper understanding of group as a part of group. Some methods, such as making group rules and clarifying task division, can be used to make a deeper connection between individuals and the group.

- *Form primary Interact*—This step is a normalization phase. The individuals in the group begin sharing information with each other, for example, discussing the course contents. Some methods, such as providing feedback on interactions, can be used to promote interaction between the groups.
- *Promote real collaboration*—This step is a real collaboration phase. The indi- viduals begin to confirm their ideas and actively reflect themselves. Some methods, such as writing reflection, can be used to enhance group members' collaboration.

**Analysis and Measure Social Learning**

The ability to measure and to appreciate the complexity of the processes of social learning has benefited from advances in methodologies and development of com- putational power.

**Social Interactions**

Individuals' interaction pattern is an important assessment element of social learning. When people interact with each other, a social network is forming. The social network is a social structure made up of individuals (or organizations) called "nodes," which are tied (connected) by one or more specific types of interdepen- dency, such as interaction, friendship, and kinship .

Assessment of social network should use a method named social network analysis. According to the constitution of social network, social network analysis usually focuses on several key terms, such as sociogram, density, centrality, in-degree, and out-degree.

*Sociogram* is the visualization to show the situation of the whole or the part of the social network. In the sociogram, the node represents the actor, the line represents the relationship between actors, and the arrow direction represents the information flow.

*Density* describes the connection degree of a network. It refers to the number of ties an actor has, divided by the total possible ties an actor. For example, if there are ten actors, each actor could potentially have nine ties that means the actor could potentially connect to other nine actors. If an actor has six ties, the density of the network is 66.67% (6/9). The bigger the number of density stands, the better the connection of the network. *Centrality* describes the numbers of ties an actor has. The more ties an actor has, the higher centrality it is. When the network has direction, there are two indicators to explain centrality: in-degree and out-degree. For example, if actor A comments on actor B, then the direction between them is A point to B, so out-degree can be used to describe actor A (because it is the one commented) and in-degree can be used to describe actor B (because it is the one who received comments). If an actor has higher in-degree, it means the actor receives more information; if an actor has higher out-degree, it means the actor provides more information.

**Case 1** Social interaction analysis of an online English-to-Chinese cooperative translation activity Analyzed the social network of online English-to-Chinese translation activity. The participants are 48 sophomores majoring in educational technology at Jiangsu Normal University. They were randomly assigned to twelve groups of four students. The network formed by the group's interaction was directed. From a sociogram, we can see each group has a connection, which means groups could communicate with other groups without obstacles.

The density of this sociogram is 0.65, which means it is a high-density network. Groups in the network are in touch with most of the other groups, and the infor- mation can flow freely among different groups.indicates that Group 4 is most active in sharing information and has a strong influence on the network. Group 2 receives the most information but has a minimum of sharing. That is to say, Group 2 is in control of other groups and has little influence on others.

### Content Analysis

When individuals interact with each other, especially discussing and chatting, the understanding of the content could become deeper within the interaction. The social interaction is usually related to knowledge building.

*Knowledge building* can be considered as a form of deep constructivism defined knowledge building as the production and continual improvement of ideas of value to a community that involves individuals and groups coming to a deeper understanding through interactive querying, discussing, and continuing improvement of ideas. It is worth noting that this notion of deep learning by educational psychologists and technologists is different from what computer scientists and artificial intelligence researchers call deep learning in the context of machine learning.

Content interaction is usually measured by content analysis, which is a method to analyze the procedures with text. The text usually includes chats, discussion boards, and log file data. The content analysis includes three steps: (1) adopting a coding scheme, (2) coding the text, (3) analyzing the results.

**Case 2** Content analysis of a collaborative inquiry learning among four elementary schools in China Zheng analyzed the final products of a collaborative inquiry activity. The participants are 196 pupils from 4 classes in four elementary schools in China. The pupils were randomly assigned to the groups of four or five.

At first, Zheng selected the coding scheme proposed by Zhang to analyze the level of knowledge building. The scheme includes scien- tificness and complexity.

In order to make sure the coding is credible, two raters coded all the discussion text independently. The raters compared the coding, and Zheng calculated the inter-rater agreement that achieved 0.91.

Finally, Zheng calculated the percent of each knowledge level.

Regarding scientificness, the result indicated that 0.4% of the discussion tran- scripts were prescientific, 1% of them were hybrid, 18.6% of them were basically scientific, and 64% of them were scientific.Concluded that most learners had acquired scientific knowledge about tools in daily life.

In complexity aspect, the result demonstrated that 16% of discourse transcripts were unelaborated facts, 67.3% of them were elaborated facts, only 0.9% of them were unelaborated explanations, and 15% of them were elaborated explanations.

Zheng concluded the finding indicated that most learners could elaborate terms, phenomena, and facts. However, only a few of them can provide elaborated explanations about tools in daily life. Zheng suggested that the teachers should provide more elaborated explanations to deepen the understanding of tools in daily life.

**Cognitive Task Analysis**

In addition to analyzing the content to be learned, it is often useful to analyze performing tasks and solve problem related to that content. Cognitive task analysis (CTA) is a well-established technique for doing such an analysis. CTA makes use of observations, interviews and talk-aloud techniques to extract both explicit and implicit experiences in solving problems and making decisions pertaining to the content to be learned. Common methods used in CTA include collecting preliminary knowledge (e.g., via document reviews), identifying relevant knowledge representations (e.g., in the form of concept maps or causal influence diagrams), applying knowledge elicitation techniques (e.g., interviews and think-aloud methods), and developing the results in a manner suitable for testing with less experienced persons. One key aspect of a cognitive task analysis is to identify key distinctions and decision points that influence what a problem solver or decision maker does.

**Group Performance**

The traditional assessment methods, such as final tests, submitting artifacts or products are adopted to analyze the group performance. Through these assessments, we can infer what they know, can do, or have accomplished in general.

A final test is a traditional method to evaluate the knowledge of learners. In the practice situation, making artifacts or products has been the standard assessment methods. The steps of product evaluating methods are similar to content analysis; both of them need to adopt an evaluation scheme. After that, products should be assessed according to the scheme.

Case Products evaluation of a collaborative inquiry learning among four elemen- tary schools in China

Zheng analyzed the final products of a collaborative inquiry activity. The participants are 196 pupils from 4 classes in 4 primary schools in China. The pupils in each class were randomly assigned to the groups of four or five. Finally, 48 groups were formed.

At first, Zheng chose the coding scheme proposed to analyze the submitted products of learning groups. The scheme includes word, space, color, and theme. Each dimension is separated into three levels .

Zheng evaluated the final products of groups according to the scheme and analyzed the means and standard deviations of group products. The results indi- cated that all of groups made great efforts to collaboratively draw the artifacts.

**Key Points in This Chapter**

1. Social learning can be considered as a change in understanding that goes beyond the individual to become situated within wider social units or com- munities of practice through social interactions between actors within social networks.

2. Benefits of social learning can be summarized into three major categories: social, psychological, and academic.

3. Features of technology in social learning can be described to promote student collaboration and knowledge creation, enhance student cognitive performance or foster deep understanding, add flexibility of time and space for social learning and promote student engagement and keep track of student collaboration.

4. The group development process can be described based on the five-stage model: forming, norming, storming, performing, and adjourning.

5. Building learning community usually includes five steps: introductions, iden- tification with the group, interaction, group cohesion and individual reflection, and expansive questioning.

6. Group performance can be measured and analyzed in three aspects, namely social interactions, content interaction, and group product.

# Learning Activities

**Introduction**

In this chapter, the focus will be first on some general principles of learning activities design and then on principles to consider when designing instructional systems.The first part of this chapter focuses on planning and implementing learning activities in accordance with Bloom's revised taxonomy , Sweller's cognitive load theory, and also Mayer's principles of multimedia learning, with the goal of developing a basic skill for the reader to design learning activities.

Instructional Design (Instructional Systems Design (ISD) is the practice of creating instructional experiences to support the development and acquisition of knowledge and skill. There are many instructional design models, and many are variants of the generic ADDIE (a model, which refers to analysis, design, development, implementation, and evaluation). Instructional design is historically and traditionally rooted in cognitive and behavioral psy- chology, and constructivism (learning theory) also has influenced thinking in the field. The second part of this chapter includes a discussion of big D (i.e., design and development considered from a life-cycle perspective; the larger-scale instructional systems development found in ADDIE).

**Learning Activity Design:Learning Activity**

Learning activity is a particular kind of human activity whose primary objective is the development of knowledge, skills, and competencies. It is produced by the society in the process of history through special learning actions taken upon learning objects consistent with their substance and structure. A learning activity is an interaction between a learner and an environment (optionally involving other learners, practitioners, resources, tools, and services) to achieve a planned learning outcome. It can be defined as specific interactions of learners with other people, using specific tools and resources, oriented toward specific outcomes.

The teacher's essential task is to get students to engage in learning activities that are likely to result in achieving outcomes. What the *student* does is more important than what the *teacher* does. Each learning activity in the course should be *intentional, meaningful, and useful.*

From the perspective of a teacher or designer, a complete learning activity consists of the following components: learning objectives, activities or tasks, learning methods and operational procedures, organizational forms, ways of interaction, forms of learning outcomes, activity monitoring rules, formative feedback, roles and responsibilities, learning evaluation rules, and evaluation cri- teria. Learning activities should include three essential elements: learning tasks, learning methods, and evaluation requirements. From the perspective of learners, each learning activity includes four aspects: learning tasks, learning resources, evaluation methods, and learning support services.

- Learning tasks require a clear description of the learning outcomes so that the learners can explicitly understand what they should do in the associated activity.
- Learning resources include both non-digital and digital materials providing the learner with the necessary information and content, for example, textbooks, study guides, journal articles and reading packets, video clips, and online resources.
- The basic principle of preparing learning resources is that they should be adequate and appropriate to complete the learning tasks with the result of reducing redundant resources.
- Evaluation methods should adequately examine the completion of learning activities without focusing on the assessment of learners' memorization of the learning contents.
- Learning support services are extremely important, so the instructors or tutors have to understand the learning difficulties and learning environment of the learners so as to facilitate effective communication with them.

There should not be too many learning activities in a unit of instruction so as to minimize the extraneous cognitive burden placed on the learners. Learning objec- tives, student's acceptance of the activity considering their cognitive load, and the various resources provided for the activity are critical points of learning activity design.

The learning objective is the starting point, and also the destination of learning activity design, while learner characteristics and resource conditions are constraints. To design learning activity better, we need to focus on some theories related to these points, such as Bloom's taxonomy, Sweller's cognitive load theory, and Mayer's principles of multimedia learning.

**Bloom's Taxonomy**

The primary purpose of learning objective analysis is to find out what learning outcome the learners can obtain after learning a specific part of the content, such as knowledge, skills, and so on. There are many ways to characterize learning objectives, and it requires a target classification framework to interpret systemati- cally. Bloom's taxonomy is a familiar classic classification framework for analyzing the learning objectives.

Benjamin developed a hierarchy of educational objectives, which is referred to as Bloom's taxonomy, which covers the learning objectives in three domains: cognitive, affective, and psychomotor.

- The cognitive domain includes intellectual skills and knowledge processing, which is the primary focus of most traditional education and is frequently used to structure curriculum learning objectives, assessments, and activities.
- The affective domain represents objectives that are concerned with attitudes and feelings.
- The psychomotor domain concerns what students might do physically.

**Cognitive Domain**

Bloom's taxonomy within the cognitive domain includes the six levels: knowledge, comprehension, application, analysis, synthesis, and evaluation. The six levels are classified hierarchically from the simplest action to the high-order thinking actions. The six levels of Bloom's taxonomy were arranged in a cumulative hierarchical framework, that is, achievement of complex skill or ability required achievement of the prior one.

1. Knowledge

   - Deals primarily with the ability to memorize and recall specific facts
   - Example: Name common varieties of apple.

2. Comprehension

- Involves the ability to interpret, and demonstrate students' basic under- standing of ideas
- Example: Compare the identifying characteristics of a Golden Delicious apple with a Granny Smith apple.

3. Application

   - Involves the ability to apply concepts and principles to novel practical situations
   - Example: Would apples prevent scurvy, a disease caused by a deficiency in vitamin C?

4. Analysis

   - Involves the ability to analyze concepts and separate concepts or principles into components
   - Example: List four ways of serving foods made with apples and explain which ones have the highest health benefits. Provide references to support your statements.

5. Synthesis

   - Involves the ability to blend elements and parts to form a whole

- Example: Convert an "unhealthy" recipe for apple pie to a "healthy" recipe by replacing your choice of ingredients. Explain the health benefits of using the ingredients you chose versus the original ones.

6. Evaluation

   - Involves the ability to make judgments of the value of a work
   - Example: Which kinds of apples are best for baking a pie, and why?

**Affective Domain**

The affective domain relates to emotions, attitudes, appreciations, and values, such as enjoying, conserving, respecting, and supporting. The affective domain is divi- ded into five main subcategories: receiving, responding, valuing, organization, and characterization.

1. Receiving

   - Students pay attention passively, and it is about the student's memory and recognition as well. Without receiving, no learning can occur.

2. Responding

   - Students participate learning process activity. They not only attend to a stimulus but also reacts in sometimes and some way.

3. Valuing

   - Students attach and associate a value or some values to an object, phe- nomenon, or piece of information, and even the knowledge they acquired.

4. Organizing

   - Students can put different values, information, and ideas and accommodate them within their schema together. They can compare, relate, and elaborate on what has been learned.

5. Characterizing

   - Students can build abstract knowledge.

**Psychomotor Domain**

Bloom has not compiled the taxonomy of the psychomotor domain, but several competing taxonomies for the psychomotor domain have been created over the years. The psychomotor domain concerns things students might physically do. One popular versions of the taxonomy for the psy- chomotor domain belongs, who presents the five levels of the psychomotor domain as imitation, manipulation, precision, articulation, and naturalization.

**Case Study**

When design learning objective, it should be specific, operational, and measurable.

**Case:** The Learning Objective of *Newton's First Law*

- Explain the content and meaning of Newton's first law (cognitive- comprehension).
- Illustrate and explain the simple phenomenon of daily life that resulted from the inertia (cognitive-

comprehension).

- Experience the difficulty of the scientific research process, and realize the experimental and reasoning scientific research methods (affective).

### Extended Reading

With the development of learning theory, scholars have revised and improved Bloom's taxonomy. Also, in the research field of objective classification, there are other scholars proposed different learning objectives' classification framework from different perspectives.

1. **Revised Taxonomy**

Bloom's taxonomy is a scheme for classifying educational goals, objectives, and standards. It provides an organizational structure and a common meaning to learning objectives classified in one of its categories.

Lorin W. Anderson and David R. Krathwohl revisited the cognitive domain in the learning taxonomy to reflect a positive form of thinking and made some changes, such as changing the names from noun to verb forms, and slightly rear- ranging them. In contrast to the single dimension of the original taxonomy, the revised framework is two-dimensional, cognitive process and knowledge dimension.

The cognitive process dimension contains six categories from cognitively simple to cognitively complex: remember, understand, apply, analyze, evaluate, and create. The knowledge dimension contains four categories from concrete to abstract: factual, conceptual, procedural, and metacognitive.

In the revised taxonomy, the cognitive process dimension has six levels that are arranged in a hierarchical structure, but not as rigidly as in the original taxonomy. In combination, the knowledge and cognitive process dimensions.

2. Gagné's taxonomy Gagné proposed five categories of learning objective: verbal information, intellectual skills, cognitive strategies, motor skills, and atti- tudes. Gagné and Bloom represent learning objectives in different aspects, that Bloom's classification is more from the "form" of the learning objectives, and Gagné's classification is mainly from the "content" point of view, and he did not subdivide affective and psychomotor domain. Gagne assumed that different types of learning outcomes required different learning conditions.

### Cognitive Load Theory

Cognitive load theory is created for letting learners get information and learning content efficient. It is an instructional theory based on the field's knowledge of human cognitive architecture and can be used to recommend in instructional procedures.

Cognitive load theory builds upon the human information processing model and placed its primary emphasis on relations between working memory and long-term memory during the 1980s and 1990s. It was developed out of the study of problem solving by John Sweller in the late 1980s, which differentiates cognitive load into three types: intrinsic, extraneous, and germane.

### Intrinsic Cognitive Load

Intrinsic cognitive load is the inherent level of difficulty associated with a specific instructional topic that cannot be altered due to the nature of the material. However, it needs to be considered in activity design so that knowledge can be communicated at the right grain size.

### Extraneous Cognitive Load

Extraneous cognitive load is generated by information presented to learners and is under the control of learning activity designers. It can be attributed to the design of the learning materials, and it can and should be altered. Unnecessary information within the text or format may cause an overload in the working memory and will affect the learner's storage of information negatively. Multiple sources of information, unnecessary and comprehensive format, extra sounds, and long complex explanations are examples of extraneous cognitive load.

### Germane Cognitive Load

Germane cognitive load is devoted to the processing, construction, and automation of schemas. It is extra information that can be altered, just like the extraneous cognitive load. As the intrinsic cognitive load is thought to be permanent, it is suggested that the learning designers should limit extraneous load and promote germane load (Sweller, Van Merriënboer, & Paas). However, germane cognitive load should be used for necessary schematic construction.

### Cognitive Load Theory with Learning Activity Design

First, in addition to short-term memory limitations, different kinds of cognitive load are distinguished. Intrinsic load is that which is inherent in the problem or situation itself and cannot be manipulated to any significant extent.

Second, the extrinsic cognitive load is that which occurs in the situation context and which might be reduced or minimized.

Third, the germane cognitive load is that which directs the learner to the essential features of the problem situation and allows some things to be ignored.

Sweller argued that working memory has a limited capacity, so instructional methods should avoid overloading it with additional activities, which do not directly contribute to learning. The learning and instructional design should be used to reduce cognitive load in learners. When intrinsic or germane load is high (i.e.,when a problem is difficult), materials should be designed to reduce the extraneous load.

In a word, cognitive load theory provides a general framework and has broad implications for learning activity design. It allows instructional designers to control the conditions of learning within an environment or, more generally, within most instructional materials. The implications for instructional design are clear:

a. Minimize extrinsic load factors in an instructional situation.
b. Help new learners focus on that which is essential without generating addi- tional extrinsic load.

### Case Study

In the stage of junior high school, the "law of inertia" is a crucial topic in relevant curriculum. It is hard for students to differentiate the concept that objects possess natural properties of uniform linear motion and stationary state from the concept of features that objects have in the inertia.

1. Intrinsic cognitive load: the law of inertia/Newton's first law
2. Extraneous cognitive load: suitable activity design or learning method
3. Germane cognitive load: Review the relevant laws, or provide different examples of Newton's first law.

### Design strategy:

1. Design physical and animation experiment presentation to reduce the intrinsic cognitive load.
2. Design a learning activity that recalls the simple phenomenon of daily life, which resulted from the inertia, for example, when the car starts or brakes suddenly, passengers will be tilted backward or forward.

### Mayer's Principles of Multimedia Learning

If you are designing resources for learning activities or creating a PowerPoint presentation for a lecture, developing an online course, preparing to flip a class- room, you may need to reconsider how you will get students to engage in the learning materials.

Mayer's cognitive theory of multimedia learning centers on the idea that learners attempt to build meaningful connections between words and pictures, which they learn more deeply than they could have with words or pictures alone (Mayer). One of the principal aims of multimedia instruction is to encourage the learner to construct a coherent mental representation of the material. The learner's job is to make sense of the presented material as an active participant, ultimately con- structing new knowledge.

**Mayer's Principles of Multimedia Learning**

Mayer identifies twelve multimedia learning or instructional principles which were developed from nearly 100 studies over the past two decades:

1. **Coherence Principle**

   People learn better when extraneous words, pictures, and sounds are excluded rather than included.

2. **Signaling Principle**

   People learn better when cues that highlight the organization of the essential material are added.

3. **Redundancy Principle**

   People learn better from graphics and narration than from graphics, narration and on-screen text.

4. **Spatial Contiguity Principle**

   People learn better when corresponding words and pictures are presented near rather than far from each other on the page or screen.

5. **Temporal Contiguity Principle**

   People learn better when corresponding words and pictures are presented simultaneously rather than successively.

6. **Segmenting Principle**

   People learn better from a multimedia lesson is presented in user-paced segments rather than as a continuous unit.

7. **Pretraining Principle**

   People learn better from a multimedia lesson when they know the names and characteristics of the main concepts.

8. **Modality Principle**

   People learn better from graphics and narrations than from animation and on-screen text.

9. **Multimedia Principle**

   People learn better from words and pictures than from words alone.

10. **Personalization Principle**

    People learn better from multimedia lessons when words are in conversational style rather than formal style.

11. **Voice Principle**

People learn better when the narration in multimedia lessons is spoken in a friendly human voice rather than a machine voice.

12. **Image Principle**

People do not necessarily learn better from a multimedia lesson when the speaker's image is added to the screen. These twelve principles can divide into three groups based on the types of cognitive load.

**Case Study**

For learning design of Newton's first law, as the content is difficult and abstract, we have to use some multimedia resources.

**Design strategy:**

1. Use flash or animation experiment presentation.
2. Use daily life examples and pictures.

**Extended Reading**

Mayer's cognitive theory of multimedia learning is based on three assumptions: the dual-channel assumption, the limited capacity assumption, and the active pro- cessing assumption (Mayer).

1. The dual-channel assumption considers that working memory has auditory and visual channels based on Baddeley's theory of working memory (Bad- deley, & Hitch) and Paivio's dual-coding theory(Paivio).
2. The limited capacity assumption is based on cognitive load theory. It states that each subsystem of working memory has a limited capacity.
3. The active processing assumption claims that people construct knowledge in meaningful ways when they pay attention to the relevant material and organize it into a coherent mental.

Mayer's cognitive theory of multimedia learning claims that words and pictures are presented to the learner via a multimedia presentation, which is processed along two separate, non-conflicting channels.Information enters the sensory memory through the ears and eyes. The learner selects words and pictures actively from the sensory memory and enters the working memory where they are organized into a verbal model and a pictorial model.

Each channel can process only a few information at a given time in working memory. Two models are then integrated with prior knowledge retrieved from long-term memory. This integration occurs within the working memory following each segmented portion of instruction offered to the learner in the multimedia presentation.

**Instructional Systems Design**

Instructional Systems Design is an iterative process of planning learning objectives, selecting instructional strategies, choosing media, and selecting or creating mate- rials and evaluation. It is characterized as learner-centered and goal-oriented, focusing on meaningful performance, assuming that outcomes can be measured,

and procedures are based on empirical evidence, interactive, self-correcting, and typically a team effort. There are many instructional design models, and many of them are based on the ADDIE model, which comprises analysis, design, devel- opment, implementation, and evaluation.

**ADDIE Model**

The ADDIE model is a framework that displays generic processes that instructional designers and training developers do (Morrison, Ross, & Kemp). It describes a process applied to instructional design to generate episodes of intentional learn- ing.

**Analysis**

The analysis is the first phase of the ADDIE Instructional Systems Design process, and its purpose is to identify the probable reasons for the absence of performance and recommend a solution. When completing the analysis phase, one should be able to determine if the instruction could bridge the performance gap, and the degree to bridge the gap, and then provide strategies to reduce the performance gap based on empirical evidence about the potential for success. The standard procedures and typical deliverable associated with the analysis phase.

1. **Validate the performance gap.**

Instructional designers are often requested to develop instruction for knowledge people already possess or skills people can already perform. The initial step in the instructional design process is to validate the performance gap and analyze the reasons or causes. The three main steps for validating the performance gap measure the actual performance, confirm the desired performance, and identify the causes of the performance gap.

Designer measures the actual performance and confirms the desired performance through observe, test, interview, and data. When the extent of the performance gap has been determined, the next step is to identify the primary cause of the gap. Practically, causes for a performance discrepancy can be categorized as a lack of resources, lack of motivation, and lack of knowledge and skill.

The procedure to validate the performance gap could be summarized in a pur- pose statement. The aim of the purpose statement is to state in brief and explicit terms the primary function of the instructional program and the context in which the instruction will occur.

Instruction may be the best response to a performance gap in the case of lack of knowledge and skill. So the essential issue of designing instruction, a course, or a curriculum for students is to cope with the knowledge and skill deficiency.

2. **Determine instructional goals.**

Determine instructional goals is to generate goals that respond to performance gaps that are caused by a lack of knowledge and skill. It describes the "terminal" tasks that students will perform at the end of the course, such as "what will students be able to do as a result of participating in this course." The classification of instructional goals (also called learning objective) and how to write instructional goals could be found in the part of learning activity design in this chapter.

3. **Confirm the intended audience.**

Confirm the intended audience is to identify the abilities, experiences, prefer- ences, and motivation of the student. The data collected will impact decisions throughout the remaining ADDIE process, which include but not limited to group identifications, general characteristics, numbers of students, location of students, experience levels, student attitudes, skills that impact potential to succeed in the learning environment.

4. **Identify required resources.**

This step is to identify all types of resources that will be required to complete the course and the entire ADDIE process. There are four types of resources, including content resources, technology resources, instructional facilities, and human resources.

5. **Determine potential delivery systems.**

The procedure is to evaluate different instructional delivery systems and rec- ommend the best option(s) that has the highest potential to close the performance gap. Conventional delivery systems include but not limited to face-to-face, computer-based learning, video, Internet-based learning management systems, and virtual reality environment.

## 6.  Compose a project/course management plan.

This step is to create a consensual document that confirms the expectations of all parties involved in the project or course plan, which may have fours phases: ini- tiation, planning, execution, and closure. When doing a project management plan, the following four sections should consider: core instructional design team mem- bers, significant constraints, schedule tasks, and final report.

### Design

Design is the second phase of the ADDIE, with the purpose to confirm the desired performances and appropriate testing methods. After completing the design phase, one should be able to prepare a set of functional specifications for closing the performance gap due to the lack of knowledge or skills.

The standard procedures and typical deliverable associated with the design phase.

## 1.  Conduct a task inventory.

Conducting a task inventory is to identify the essential tasks required to achieve an instructional goal. A task inventory organizes the content so that the students can construct the knowledge and skills necessary to achieve the instructional goals.

The instructional design procedure is often referred to as task analysis, and a course may contain many learning tasks that facilitate students to achieve the instructional goals.

The four steps for conducting a task inventory are: repeat the purpose statement, reaffirm the instructional goals, identify the primary performance tasks, and specify prerequisite knowledge and skills.

## 2.  Compose performance objectives.

The aim of this step is to compose objectives that are congruent with the instructional goals. An objective provides a way to evaluate when a specific desired performance has been attained. Categories of learning (such as Bloom's Taxonomy) can be used to specify learning outcomes.

## 3.  Generate testing strategies.

The aim of this step to create items to test students' achievements. Testing strategies should have high fidelity between the task, the objective, and the test items. Test items should be authentic and simulate performance space.

## 4.  Calculate return on investment.

Calculate return on investment is to estimate the cost for completing the entire ADDIE process. The procedure for calculating includes calculating the training costs, the benefits derived from the training, and comparing the training benefits to the training costs. This can be considered a partial form of summative evaluation of the entire effort.

### Develop

Develop is the third phase of the ADDIE instructional design process, with the purpose to generate and validate the learning resources that will be required during the life of the instructional modules. After completing the develop phase, one should be able to identify all of the resources that will be needed to undertake the planned episodes of intentional learning.

Also, one should also have selected or developed tools to implement the planned instruction, to evaluate the instructional outcomes, and to complete the remaining phases of the ADDIE instructional design process.The main procedures and typical deliverable associated with the develop phase.

## 1.  Generate content.

The aim of this step is to generate learning plans. Content is the focal point for engaging students during the process of knowledge construction. However, content should be strategically introduced during the teaching and learning sessions. Thus instructional strategies become the overt means by which knowledge, skills, and procedures are exchanged during an episode of intentional learning.

## 2.  Select or develop supporting media.

The aim of this step is to select or develop media sufficient to accomplish the performance objective(s) as well as the remaining ADDIE procedures. Effective media facilitates the construction and retention of knowledge and skills. Instruc- tional media are intended to enrich the learning experience by using a variety of tangible items to facilitate the performance objectives. Media should be chosen to support an instructional event. Do not choose instructional events to support a medium. All of the events of instruction should be mediated, although a single episode may have different types of media. Select or develop supporting media should consider learners' cognitive load and Mayer's principles of multimedia learning media.

## 3.  Develop guidance for the student.

The aim of this step is to provide information to guide the student through the instruction. Providing guidance for navigating the instructional strategies enhances the learning experience. The format of the guiding artifact will vary depending on the instructional goals and the primary delivery system.

## 4.  Develop guidance for the teacher

The aim of this step is to provide information to guide the teacher as he or she facilitates the episodes of intentional learning. Guiding artifacts reflect the designer's selection of tasks to be performed by the students, the definition of objectives to be fulfilled, the selection of instructional strategies, and determination on the pace of instruction. This section focuses on the elements that enable the teacher to guide the student through the planned instructional strategies.

## 5.  Conduct formative revisions.

The aim of this step is to revise the instructional products and processes before implementation. Instructional designers use evaluation for the specific purpose of improving the designed instruction so that it can fulfill its goal of reducing the performance gap.

**There are two main types of evaluation used in the ADDIE approach:**

- Formative evaluation is the process of collecting data that can be used to revise the instruction plan before implementation.
- Summative evaluation is the process of collecting data following implementation.

### Implement

Implement is the fourth phase of the ADDIE instructional design process, with the purpose to prepare the learning environments and engage the students. After completing the implement phase, one should be able to work in an actual learning environment where the student can construct the new knowledge and skills. Most ADDIE approaches use the implement phase to transition the summative evaluation activities and other strategies that place into action the teaching and learning process.The standard procedures and typical deliverable associated with the implement phase.

**1. Prepare the teacher.**

The aim of this phase is to identify and prepare teachers to facilitate the instructional strategies and the learning resources that have been newly developed.

**2. Prepare the student.**

Identify and prepare students to actively participate in the instruction and effectively interact with the newly developed learning resources.

### Evaluate

Evaluate is the fifth phase of the ADDIE instructional design process, with the purpose to assess the quality of learning materials before and after implementation and to evaluate the instructional design procedures used to generate the instruc- tional products.

Evaluation of instructional design focuses on measuring the student's ability to perform her or his newly constructed knowledge and skills in an authentic work environment.The standard procedures and typical deliverable associated with the evaluation phase.

**1. Determine evaluation criteria.**

The aim of this step is to identify perception, learning, and performance as the three main levels of evaluation associated with the instructional design. The ADDIE approach to instructional design in this book promotes three levels of evaluation. Level 1 measures such things as the students' perceptions of the course content, resources used throughout the course, the comfort of the physical classroom environment, or the ease of navigation in a virtual classroom environment and the teacher's facilitation style. Level 2 evaluation measures learning that the student's ability to perform the tasks indicated in each of the goals and objectives. Level 3 evaluation measures job performance that student's knowledge and skill as they are actually applied in an authentic work environment.

**2. Select evaluation tools.**

There are a variety of measurement tools that are available to instructional designers. Each measurement tool has the attributes that render its effective for certain types of evaluation. A sample of evaluation tools includes but is not limited to questionnaire, interview, Likert scale, open-ended questions, survey, examina- tions, role-plays, observations, practice, simulations, authentic work tasks, perfor- mance checklists, supervisor assessments, peer reviews, and observations.

### Extended Reading

There are many other instructional design models from different perspectives, for example, the 4C/ID model which is particularly well suited for planning instructional systems in support of complex and ill-structured learning tasks. Tennyson's model is based on what designers actually do and reflects the dynamic and complex nature of instructional design. In addition, new models are emerging that highlight the role of collaboration, co-construction of understanding, and team problem solving.

**The Four-Component Instructional Design Model**

The four-component instructional design model (4C/ID) developed by van Mer- riënboer. The 4C/ID instructional model is characterized by four compo- nents: (1) learning tasks, (2) supportive information, (3) procedural information, and (4) part-task practice. Tasks are ordered by task difficulty, and each task is offered at the beginning a lot of scaffolding which will be reduced as the learner progresses.

The relationship of the four basic components to the associated steps involved in complex learning (van Merriënboer & Kirschner). According to van Merriënboer, the 4C/ID model addresses at least three deficits in previous instructional design models.

- First, the 4C/ID model focuses on the integration and coordinated performance of task-specific constituent skills rather than on knowledge types, context, or presentation-delivery media.
- Second, the model makes a critical distinction between supportive information and required just-in-time information (the latter specifies the performance required, not only the type of knowledge required).
- Third, traditional models use either part-task or whole-task practice; the 4C/ID model recommends a mixture where part-task practice supports very complex,"whole-task" learning.

**Tennyson's Fourth-Generation ISD Model**

The complexity of instructional design is evident in the Fourth-Generation Instructional Systems Design (ISD-4) model developed by Tennyson. Tennyson's ISD-4 model is based on a synthesis of what instructional designers actually do.

The first component in ISD-4 is the situational evaluation. The purpose of this evaluation is twofold: Assess the learning problem/need (an interface between the ID author and the problem/need) and construct ID solution plan (a plan that pro- poses an instructional development process with an appropriate set of ISD activities).

It emphasizes the notions of a situational evaluation and the fact that instruc- tional designers do not always start with analysis; the specific situation and cir- cumstances determine to a large extent what designers actually.

**Emerging Models**

Social networking and collaborative learning bring new aspects to the traditional instructional design models presented above. While the models elaborated above are well-established and can be modified to accommodate new communication technologies, it is worth noting that among the new models that are appearing in computer-supported collaborative learning, problem-based learning approaches, MOOCs, and other recent developments, one still finds the need to understand the nature of what is to be learned, who the learners are, and how progress will be determined. One exception is perhaps in the case of informal learning in which there may not be a well-defined learning goal.

**Key Points in This Chapter**

1. A learning activity is an interaction between a learner and an environment (optionally involving other learners, practitioners, resources, tools, and ser- vices) to achieve a planned learning outcome
2. Bloom's taxonomy that attempts to cover the learning objectives in cognitive, affective, and psychomotor domains. Cognitive domain represents the intel- lectual skills and knowledge processing, which is the primary focus of most traditional education and is frequently used to structure curriculum learning objectives, assessments, and activities. Affective domain represents objectives that are concerned with attitudes and feelings. Psychomotor domain concerns what students might do physically.
3. The ADDIE model is a framework that displays generic processes that instructional designers and training developers do, which describes a process applied to instructional design to generate episodes of intentional learning.

# Space Design

**Introduction**

Learning is changing in the twenty-first century. Learning happens in classrooms, homes, communities, and indoor and outdoor settings. The design of a learning space is important for desirable learning outcomes. Furthermore, technology has evolved and transformed our lives and society and learning space is enhanced by current high-quality technologies, such as interactive tutorials, wireless networks, whiteboards, and mobile devices. Maximizing student's learning is a top priority in designing or redesigning a learning space. Well-designed learning spaces support pedagogical practices that engage, challenge, and equip students with the knowl- edge, skills, and attributes they need to succeed in a complex and rapidly changing world.

This chapter will present the definition of a learning space and discuss how to evaluate learning spaces. In addition, the discussion will focus on how technology has enabled the implementation of learning spaces, in particular the usage of smart technologies.

**Learning Spaces**

Previous learning spaces mainly occurred outdoors, such as in a forest. For example, the later Xiang Order (circa 1046—256 BCE), which included private schools, academies and outdoor venues as well as the Imperial College in China. The modern learning environment appeared after the *class teaching system* pre- sented by Comenius in the sixteenth century in what is now called the Czech Republic. Since the 1990s, many new information technologies (e.g., multimedia, com- puters, digital projector, the Internet, courseware, network-based courses, tutorial Web sites and more) have entered into schools and classrooms. Learning spaces now constitute an emerging research area. The goal of a learning space is to promote independent, flexible, and engaged learning by providing learners with appropriate technologies and pedagogies. How to design and develop an effective learning space has thus become increasingly critical.

**Definition of Learning Space**

Learning space refers to a place and the surroundings associated with that place where teaching and learning occur; it may refer to an indoor or outdoor location, or to a physical or virtual environment.Formal learning is typically organized and structured and has learning objectives; formal learning is normally delivered by trained teachers in a systematic and intentional ways within a school or university.Informal learning is any learning that has no set objective in terms of learning outcomes and is never intentional from learner's standpoint, such as self-directed learning or learning from experience, (OECD) which usually occurs in learning commons, multimedia sandbox, and residential study areas.

For both formal and informal learning, virtual learning environment refers to the kind of platform that supports mediated exchange of information between users and the system through such digital media as learning management systems, social media Web sites, and online virtual classrooms and environments.

Learning spaces are designed to support, facilitate, stimulate, or enhance learning, and teaching. A learning space can be designed to support listening and taking notes (e.g., a lecture hall or traditional classroom). New technologies have added to the complexity of designing effective learning spaces and now require careful consideration of the pedagogy to supported learning. The characteristics of a learning space and its components include many variables, such as size, forms, shapes, environmental setting, technologies involved, intended activities and users, and so on.

**The Pedagogy-Space-Technology (PST) Framework**

Creating a learning space that could be used to encourage students to become actively engaged, independent, lifelong learners is a chief aim of twentieth-century pedagogy and a challenge for the design of learning spaces. The point here is that there are connections between pedagogy, technology, and the design of a learning space. These connections are evident in the TPACK (technological pedagogical content knowledge) framework (Koehler & Mishra). There are a number of relationships among these connections which are elaborated later in line with the Pedagogy-Space-Technology (PST) framework .

The sequencing of items in the PST framework (Fig.9.1) is important. Each of the three elements (pedagogy, space, and technology) influences each other in a reciprocal manner. For example, a desired pedagogy suggests a preferred way to arrange and use the space. In addition, a particular technology to be deployed may better fit some pedagogies and arrangements of the space than other possibilities. A particular space places constraints (or presents opportunities) on the introduction of certain types of technology while a given technology can impact how a space is used by teachers and students. In addition, the content to be learned and the students themselves need to be taken into account.

Given the complexity and challenges of designing effective learning spaces that take into account the content, the learners, along with the pedagogy and technology involved, an iterative planning cycle that supports refinement and evaluation is often appropriate. Iterating through the PST framework several times during planning, development and the subsequent life cycle of a learning space is likely to have desirable outcomes; that is to say, think of PST as a cradle-to-grave frame- work. While only two life-cycle stages are represented (as the columns Conception and Design and Implementation and Operation), the framework could be made more fine grained by splitting these into more than two columns corresponding to more life-cycle stages and writing appropriate questions for each stage. In addition, later stages could be added. Thus if a particular insti- tution has a prescribed set of project stages with decision points (a.k.a., key milestones), then the basic PST framework questions can be rewritten to suit the declared delivery steps or key decision stages for the institution; PST can be tai- lored to meet particular ways of doing work.

### Principles for Learning Space Design

In this section, a number of principles to guide the effective design of learning spaces are discussed. The first consideration, however, is to focus on the use of the learning space, namely the activities to be supported in the space.

### Linking Activities to a Learning Space

Multimodal learning settings can be collocated and clustered to allow in a space to fit the learning activities targeting those technologies. Some technologies and activities are useful in a wide variety of activities that make such clustering difficult.

### Principles to Guide Design

The following principles constitute a high-level strategic guide for the design of new schools, the redevelopment of schools, and the repurposing of buildings and learning spaces to maximize student performance.

### Sustainable the space should be designed to be sustainable

- Enable a space to be easily reallocated and reconfigured.
- Consider cost-effective items, utilities, delivery, and support.
- Think ahead of future development of technologies, pedagogies, and uses.
- Personalized—the space should be personalized for students and teachers
- Consider alternative and creative colors, sounds, pictures, and videos.
- Involve students and teachers in making choices to promote personalization.
- Use things that allow individual control and manipulation by students and teachers.
- Accessible the space should be open and easily available for use by all
- Use technologies that are easily moved to fit changing needs.
- Use interactive work surfaces linked to mobile devices and notebooks.
- Provide affordable access to online digital resources, services, and storage.

### Collaborative

- Provide a space to support cooperative learning and group work when those pedagogies are involved.
- Support relevant local, national, and global networks, partnerships, and learning communities.

### Engaging

- ○ Community, professional, and expert engagement.
- ○ To energize and inspire learners and tutors.
- ○ Faster, deeper learning.
- ○ Examples of Effective Learning Spaces

**Collaboration Rooms at Texas State University**

These new rooms at Texas State University are on Alkek's main floor to the right of the cafe, behind the marble wall. Student could bring laptops (Mac & PC compatible) and share screen. The following items indicate how collaboration rooms at Texas State University satisfy some of the design principles mentioned above.

- **Accessible:** According to the introduction about collaboration room, four rooms have teaching available with large monitors and power charging capability. Student can use mobile devices and notebooks to share screen.
- **Collaborative:** Collaboration room provides a space to support cooperative

learning and group work for local students; furthermore, students can also have a group discussion with global students with the help of network.

**Beijing National Day School of India**

The Beijing National Day School (BNDS), originally a school for children of the Central Military Committee, was established in 1952 and ranks as one of the biggest secondary schools in the urban area of Beijing. BNDS embraces the Maker Movement pedagogy on a large and comprehensive scale. Students design, develop, and market a variety of products associated with various subjects. VR and collaboration are evident throughout the school which typically has laboratories and workplaces rather than traditional classrooms. Sample arrangements of learning spaces at BNDS.

**Future Learning Environments in Sweden**

This design is part of a project called future learning environments for the Karolinska Institute in Sweden, grounded on research on learning and higher education.Such facilities are located primarily next to the lecture halls and were initially leftover and deserted areas. The idea is to create a *home away from home*, a natural meeting place for students, teachers, and researchers. The following items indicate how the future learning environment satisfies some of the design principles previously mentioned.

- Engaging: The facilities have become a social arena where you hang out and socialize, including a common meeting place and a central information point. The spaces include open squares, room in rooms, and reading areas for focused study.
- Collaborative: As a part of the concept of the "Home away from home", it is a place where you can exchange thoughts and ideas and where peer learning is facilitated.

With high-quality teaching resources, the 101 VR Classroom integrates virtual reality into teaching and learning, which can create a close-to-real learning envi- ronment for students. The 101 VR Classroom is an open, interactive, immerse learning environment with an accompanying editor to allow designers and teachers to create specific learning resources. The 101 VR Classroom has these characteristics.

The following items indicate how the 101 VR Classroom satisfies some of the design principles mentioned above.

- **Sustainable:** integration including e-books, teaching materials, international top education products, 3D teaching resources and other educational resources, through the mobile Internet, education cloud platform, and other technologies, with the global educators and learners to share.
- **Personalized:** In the 101 VR Classroom, the student's vision, hearing and external isolation, completely eliminate the outside interference, and completely devoted into the virtual reality, consequently achieving immerse feeling.
- **Accessible:** The students can obtain the same feeling from the real world as that from the visual, auditory, and tactile devices with the special VR equipment, span the limitation of time space, visualize the concept of

abstraction, and experience a highly open, interactive and immerse three-dimensional learning environment.

- **Engaging:** Through the visual, voice, touch, gestures, movements and even the brain waves, such as the combination of "multimode" interactive way, teachers can use VR 101 Assistant, a key device to control the class of VR equipment playback and stop, thoroughly break through the interaction between human– computer interaction, the two-dimensional interaction limitations, so that teachers can deliver more efficient teaching, and students receive more natural and easy learning.

**Smart Learning Environments**

With the development of ICT in education, researchers have begun to conceptualize how learning environments can be made more effective, efficient, and engaging on a large and sustainable scale. Smart learning environments (SLE) are defined as physical environments that are enriched with digital, context-aware, and adaptive devices to promote better and faster learning. With tech- nology support, smart classrooms become places where teachers and students can have rich and immerse teaching and learning experiences not previously possible. Hwang presented the definition and criteria of SLE from the perspective of context-aware ubiquitous learning. Hwang also introduced a framework to address the design and development of SLE to support both online and real-world learning activities with the following principles:

1. Smart learning environments should integrate a physical environment and a virtual environment. In a smart learning environment, the perceptual, moni- toring, and regulating functions of a physical environment are further enhanced. The application of augmented reality can create a seamless inte- gration of virtual environment and physical environment.
2. Smart learning environments should provide better learning support and ser- vices according to the individual characteristics of learners. Smart learning environments emphasize the process record, personalized assessment, and evaluation of effects and content delivery of learners' learning. According to the learner model, it plays a significant role in planning, monitoring, and evaluation in the development learner's learning capabilities.
3. Smart learning environments should support on-campus learning and off-campus learning, formal learning, and informal learning. The learners in this situation are not only campus learners, but also all people that have requirements of learning in their work.

### Key Features of Smart Learning Environments

In the information age, the classroom environment is changing in ways to optimize learning with new technologies and alternative pedagogical approaches. The smart classroom is one of the significant changes in which the intelligence of classroom involves five dimensions: showing, manageable, accessible, real-time interactive, and testing .

- **Showing:** The ways it presents can match learner's cognitive characteristics. The content presentation mainly characterizes the intelligence classroom information presentation ability, not only requesting the present content to be able to be visible clearly, but also demanding the present content suitable for learner's cognitive characteristic. These help enhance learner's understanding and processing of to study materials.
- **Manageable:** The flexible layout supports teaching activities. Environmental

management mainly characterizes the layout diversity and management con- venience of smart classrooms. All the equipment, systems, and resources of the classroom should have a strong manageability, including classroom layout management, equipment management, physical environment management, electrical safety management, network management.

- **Accessible:** The abundant resources are helpful in transferring various ways of learning into practice. Resource acquisition is mainly characterized with the ability of resource acquisition and the convenience of equipment access in the classroom, involving three aspects of resource selection, content distribution, and access speed.

- **Real-time Interactive:** The deep-level interaction is helpful in discovering problems and providing timely feedback. Timely interaction is mainly charac- terized by the ability of smart classrooms to support teaching interaction and interpersonal interaction, involving three aspects of facilitation, smooth inter- action, and interactive tracking.
- **Testing:** The ability to perceive the physical environment and learning behaviors is the basis for a smart classroom. Situational perception mainly characterizes the perceptual ability of the physical environment and learning behavior of the smart classroom.

### The Constituent Elements of Smart Learning Environments

The constituent elements of smart learning environments include six components resources, tools, learning communities, teaching commu- nity, learning ways, and teaching ways.

- Smart learning environments mainly consist of six elements of learning, namely resources, intelligent tools, learning community, teaching community, learning ways, and teaching ways.
- Learners and teachers interrelate and interact with the other four elements in teaching and learning, so as to promote the effective learning of learners. If learning and teaching were removed, smart learning environments cannot be regarded as learning environments.
- The occurrence of effective learning is the mutual result of individual knowledge construction and group knowledge construction. Learning community emphasizes interaction, collaboration, and exchange of learners, while teaching community is a continuum where teachers learn together, work collaboratively to pursue continuing professional development.
- Learning resources and intelligent tools provide support of both learning community and teaching community. The development of learning community and teaching community is inseparable from the mutual effects of resources and tools. All kinds of intelligent tools provide comprehensive support of the "in- telligence" of the learning environments. At the same time, learning community and teaching community advance the evolution of resources and tools.

### Main Points in This Chapter

1. Learning space refers to a place where teaching and learning occur; it may refer to an indoor or outdoor location, or to a physical or virtual environment.
2. The Pedagogy-Space-Technology (PST) framework to describe the connec- tions between pedagogy, technology and the design of a learning space as well as design process includes the three elements of pedagogy, technology, and space.
3. SPACE is a broad term to describe guide for the design of new schools, the redevelopment of schools, and the repurposing of buildings and learning spaces to maximize student performance.
4. The principles of SPACE include sustainable which means the space should be designed to be sustainable, personalized which means the space should be personalized for students and teachers, accessible which means the space should be open and easily available for use by all, collaborative which means the space should support collaboration when appropriate.
5. Smart learning environments (SLE) are defined as physical environments that are enriched with digital, context-aware, and adaptive devices to promote better and faster learning which can make learning environments more effective.
6. Key features of SLE include showing, manageable, accessible, real-time interactive and testing.
7. Six elements of SLE include resources, tools, learning communities, teaching community, learning ways, and teaching ways.

# Project Design

**Introduction**

Nowadays, the available and affordable resources and technologies which could support learning and instruction are plentiful. However, choosing the best resources for instruction in various situations is an increasingly challenging task for designers, teachers, administrators, and so on. According to Spector and Yuen, the use of educational technology requires attention to (a) effective and efficient design, development, and deployment and (b) providing the best results for the relevant constituencies. In terms of how to make sure the educational technology is best used, the educational project design and evaluation provide an innovative approach to dealing with educational problems.

In this chapter, we will introduce the concept of educational project, the methods to design educational project, and the model to evaluate educational project. The purpose of this chapter is to help develop the capacity of the instructor to use project approach to fix the problems of education.

**Educational Project Definitions**

In universities, national education departments, or local school districts, there are lots of research or development projects, which show that using of project approach to solve educational problems is an essential method used by researchers and teachers. A project is a series of activities or a structure aimed at bringing about clearly specified objectives within a given time and budget. So as to educational project, the goals and objectives, budget and times, and clear beginning and ending should be considered.

Educational project can be defined as a planned effort to bring about desired educational outcomes that have a budget, resources, a definite beginning, a dura- tion, and reasonably well-defined goals and objectives.

**Characters of Educational Project**

According to the definition of educational project, we can know some characters of educational project, such as desired educational outcomes, clearly start and end, and well-defined goals and objectives. In order to achieve viability and sustainability, a development educational project, regardless of its size and extension, should be oriented to the following characteristics:

- The starting point of a project is the existence of a problem affecting a certain group.
- A project is a participatory exercise from start to end.
- A well-defined project is result-based.
- Being result-based, a project seeks clearly defined objectives or outcomes, and it includes a series of interrelated and coordinated activities.
- Whereas the problem is the project's starting point, the objectives are the end point.
- Project implementation is organized with a fixed budget, limited resources, and specific deadlines.
- Each project has a specific management structure.
- Each project includes a monitoring and evaluation (M&E) system.
- A project has to be sustainable in relation to society, finance, institution, and environment.
- Finally, each project is unique.

**Life Cycle of Educational Project**

Every project must follow a series of phases, allowing the process to be booted before the problem is identified until it is resolved. This series of phases is known as the life cycle of project . Project life cycle generally involves:

(1) tasks completed at each stage or substage and (2) the team responsible for each of the phases defined (Prabhakar), depicts a typical project cycle which is somewhat familiar to the instructional design model presented in a pre- vious chapter.

**Initiating Processes**

The initiating processes determine the nature and scope of the project. The main purpose is understanding the situation of projects through analyzing the business needs/requirements in measurable goals, reviewing the current operations, and analyzing stakeholder input (including users and support personnel for the project).

**Planning Processes**

After the initiation stage, the project is planned to an appropriate level of detail. The main purpose is to plan time, cost, and resources adequately to estimate the work needed and to manage risk effectively during project execution. Planning is an ongoing effort throughout the life of the project.

**Executing Processes**

The executing phase ensures that the project management plans prepared at the planning stage are executed accordingly. This phase involves proper human resources, financial resources, and time arrangements. The output of this phase is the project deliverables.

**Controlling Processes**

Project performance must be monitored and measured regularly to identify the outcomes from the plan. Controlling processes ensure the project objectives are met by monitoring and measuring progress regularly to identify outcomes from the plan so that corrective action can be taken when necessary. Controlling process also includes taking preventive action in anticipation of possible problems.

**Closing Processes**

This is generally conducted at the end of the project to see whether the planned benefits were achieved. Lessons learned are underlined and could be documented so that they can be replicated or scaled up and integrated into future cooperative development strategies and projects.

**Design of an Educational Project**

**Logic Models**

When planning educational projects, sometimes it needs to have a visual repre- sentation with the textual explanation together to illustrate the effort, the nature of the situation, the choice of a particular solution, and the expectation of specific results of the effort. The visual representation can be called as a logic model. When designing an educational project, we should know what kind of problems to solve, what kind of effort would be applied, and what results would be achieved. In other words, we should know the goals, inputs, outputs, and outcomes.

**Goals**

A project has a goal and objectives, a beginning and an ending. The beginning could be analyzing problems and setting goals. The goals usually come from problems in the situation. Thus, the first thing we need to do is problem analysis. Every project aims to help solve a problem. The problem analysis can identify the negative aspects of the existing situation and establish a cause and effect relationship between the likely underlying causes of the problems in the situation. However, not all negative aspects are a problem. Each problem has a symptom that needs to be identified. The so-called symptoms refer to certain conditions, pro- cesses, feelings, or other phenomena or situations. Just like a person may have a headache because of a cold or it may be due to overwork. The headache is a symptom, and the cause of headache is the problem. Symptoms can be seen as a sign or indication of the problem. Spector and Yuan described a simplified problem analysis process,):

**Step One:**Use all the facts and available data to describe the problem symptoms. Select the most important problem symptom and ask: What happened? What is happening? What are the specific symptoms? Why does this happen? Identify any emerging pattern.

**Step Two:**Record and compile possible explanations and ask: What proof do we have to prove that the problem exists? What is the impact of the problem?

**Step Three:**Continue step one and step two until the explanation converges to some basic causal factors. Concern about the systemic interpretation and ask: What sequence of events led to the problem? What conditions allow the problem to happen? What other issues center around the occurrence of central problems?

**Step Four:**Define the problem or problems by describing their root causes. Determine the system structure relationship that is creating the conditions that need to be corrected and ask: Why do causal factors exist? What is the real cause of the problem?

**Step Five:**Determine the action or actions required to change the system relationship that created the problem or problems. Suggest implementing a solution and ask: How will the solution be achieved? Who is responsible? What are the risks of imple- menting the solution?

When problem or problems are ensured, the goals or objectives are also emerged. The goals or objectives can be thought as the situation in the future, once problems have been resolved. The negative situations of the problem are converted into solutions and expressed as positive achievements of the objective.

**Input Factors**

To implement a project, input factors are necessary. Inputs typically include such things as resources required and obtained, training materials developed, training provided, results of quality reviews and small-scale field tests.

A resource (input) plan helps to present all the materials and resources needed for project implementation. It lays down the requirements for staff, equipment and materials, and budgeting, and provides the cost of the required resources. The resource plan lists the requirements and costs of all necessary inputs: personnel, basic office premises or facilities, equipment and materials, or services such as special subcontracting supplies, training workshops.Resource (input) plans need to be tailored to specific activities and actions. For each activity, a list of inputs is prepared, which can then be aggregated by category to prepare an overall project resource plan sample of resource plan.

**Outputs**

In order to achieve the goals of the project, many activities or action needs to be set up. The outputs are the products of the activities. An output has to be: (1) delivered by the project, (2) demand-driven and not supply-led, (3) stated clearly in verifiable terms, and (4) feasible with the available budget.

The outputs are achieved by setting measurable indicators. Indicators are an objective measure of whether and to what extent progress has been made (related to project objectives and outputs). Performance indicators usually need to be at the output level. And indicators of output should not be a summary of what has been stated at the activities, but rather a measurable result of the execution of the activity.

When developing the indicators of outputs, the verification methods also need to be considered and designated. This will help test whether the indicators can actually be measured with reasonable time, money, and effort or not.

**The means of verification should specify:**

- How to collect the information (e.g., from video records, sample surveys, observation,) and/or the available documented source (e.g., final products).
- Who should collect/provide the information (e.g., local government workers, contracted survey teams, the project management team).
- When information should be collected (e.g., monthly, quarterly, annually).

Outcomes

The outcomes are often divided into short-, medium-, and long-term outcomes. The short-term and medium-term outcomes are usually linked directly to the goal of the effort or the specific problem situation that drives the effort. For example, the problem is that too many high school students did not go to college to continue their studies. Then, the short- or medium-term result of this effort is to increase the rate of enrollmentperhaps by 15% in the short term and 30% in the long term.

There are two points to emphasize at short-term and medium-term outcomes. First, the short and medium-term outcomes should be directly and clearly linked to the situation of the problem and the goal of the effort. Second, the short- and medium-term outcomes are usually measured, like outputs. However, long-term outcomes are often unmeasurable for a variety of reasons. In education, the long-term outcomes might increase the quality of national population, the rate of employment in a particular field, or the rate of postgraduate entrancement. Those long-term outcomes can benefit the interest to the institution or to society. However, measuring these long-term results.

**A Representative Logic Model**

Some of the ideas presented in this chapter will be new to many readers. To help make the process of developing a logic model to guide design, development, and deployment of an educational project, an actual case is presented in abbreviated form next. This case involved a multi-year effort in a large school district with about 40 schools and nearly 50,000 students to redo the entire computing infrastructure of the district so as to be able to implement personalized and adaptive learning throughout the school district. Needless to say, this was a very large project with many different stakeholders, including administrators, staff, teachers, students, and parents. It was evident at the beginning of the effort that key administrators and many teachers were enthusiastic about the effort. However, since such an effort would eventually involve all teachers as the key implementers of what was being developed, emphasis would be placed on strong and ongoing support for teachers, including a series of training sessions as the effort evolved.

In addition, it was imagined that some teachers would resist the dramatic changes planned. As a consequence, to gain support from all teachers, the first-year effort was devoted to addressing the concerns teachers had with the existing computer systems—primarily issues involving the student information system. Such things as a requirement for multiple log-ins to different parts of the system and duplicate entry of student data were reported and addressed first in an effort to gain widespread support for subsequent efforts that would affect teaching activities— namely creating individual learning plans for each learner that were previously only required for learners with disabilities. Special care was taken to automate and support as much of that new task as possible while helping teachers to adjust to new roles shifting from primary disseminators of information to coaches helping indi- vidual learners develop understanding.

A generic logic model and an actual logic model that was initially developed for the project described above are depicted. While a logic model is intended to depict what is being done in an educational project, the model is usually complemented with a description of the rationale for the effort, which is called a theory of change. As a simple example, suppose a game is being designed and developed to help young learners understand how plants are classified. An initial analysis of the problem situation might have suggested that students find the subject boring and do not spend sufficient time practicing clas- sifying various examples. Research strongly suggests that the time spent on a learning task and that timely, informative feedback tend to improve learning per- formance. A game can potentially engage learners so that they are spending more time practicing albeit in the form of a game, and the game can also provide immediate feedback. Such a rationale becomes part of a theory of change, creating in effect a chain that goes from motivation to more time learning and more feedback to improved learning outcomes.

**Evaluation of Educational Project**

The purpose to evaluate the project is to conduct a comprehensive assessment of the completed project, to determine the relevance, effectiveness, efficiency, impact, and sustainability of the project to achieve the goal.

According to the logical framework, evaluation can be adapted in four aspects: context evaluation, input evaluation, process evaluation, and product evaluation. This evaluation model is named CIPP evaluation model developed by Daniel Stufflebeam and colleagues.

Delineating refers to the delineation of questions to be answered and the information obtained; obtaining refers to obtaining relevant information; providing refers to the provision of information to decision makers so that they can use it to make decisions and thereby to improve ongoing plans. The horizontal dimension includes four kinds of evaluation: context, input, process, and product (Stufflebeam).

Context evaluation provides information about the strengths and weaknesses of a total system to assist in planning improvement-oriented objectives at each level of the system (Stufflebeam). The content usually refers to understanding the relevant environment; diagnosing special problems; analyzing training needs; determining requirements; and setting project goals.

Input evaluation provides information about the strengths and weaknesses of alternative strategies which might be chosen and structured for the achievement of given objectives (Stufflebeam). Input evaluation includes collecting training resource information; assessing training resources; determining how to effectively use existing resources to achieve training objectives; and determining whether the overall strategy for project planning and design requires the assistance of external resources.

Process evaluation provides information about the strengths and weaknesses of a chosen strategy under conditions of actual implementation, so that either the strategy or its implementation might be strengthened (Stufflebeam). The purpose of the process evaluation is to provide information feedback to constantly modify or improve the implementation process of the project. Process evaluation is mainly achieved through the ways as insight into the potential causes of failures in the implementation process; suggestions for eliminating potential failures; analysis of unfavorable factors leading to failures in the implementation process; and methods for overcoming unfavorable factors.

Product evaluation provides information for determining whether objectives or goals are being achieved and whether the change procedure which has been employed to achieve them should be continued, modified, or terminated (Stuf- flebeam). The main task of the product evaluation is to measure and explain the objectives of goals achieved by the activities of project, including both the measurement and the interpretation of the achieved goals.

Evaluation, based on the indicators, focuses on the project's implementation process and how the project contributes to the goals. Evaluation is the last step of the project cycle, but it is not the end of a project. Indeed, it can be considered the starting point for a new planning process, because the conclusions of the evaluation will allow the stakeholders to draw lessons that may guide future decision making and project identification.

**Key Points in This Chapter**

1. An educational project is a planned effort to bring about desired educational outcomes, which has a budget, resources, a definite beginning, a duration, and reasonably well-defined goals and objectives.
2. Every project has to follow a series of phases, allowing the process to be guided from the moment the problem is identified until it is solved. This series of phases is known as the life cycle of project, including initiating processes, planning processes, executing processes, and controlling processes.
3. The first step in the design phase is the identification goals of the project. The methodology used is called situation analysis. To prepare a result-based project, the following will have to be performed: (1) problem analysis and (2) objective analysis.
4. Typical structure of a logical framework includes: (a) key aspects of the current situation, (b) activities associated with the effort (inputs), (c) the anticipated results of those activities (outputs), and (d) short-, medium-, and long-term outcomes of the effort.
5. The CIPP evaluation model includes two key dimensions. The vertical dimension includes the three steps in the evaluation process called delineating, obtaining, and providing: delineating questions to be answered and information to be obtained, obtaining relevant information, and providing information to decision makers.

# Research Dimension

**Introduction**

There are two main types of educational research. The first is basic research, which is also referred to as an academic research approach. The second type is applied research (or contract research). Both of these research types have different purposes which influence the nature of the respective research.

The basis for educational research is the scientific method. The scientific method uses directed questions and manipulation of variables to systematically find infor- mation about the teaching and learning process. This scenario questions are answered by the analysis of data that are collected specifically for the purpose to answer these questions. The two main types of data that are used under this method are qualitative and quantitative.

Qualitative research uses data which are descriptive in nature. Tools that edu- cational researchers use in collecting qualitative data include observations, con- ducting interviews, conducting document analysis, and analyzing participant products such as journals, diaries, images, or blogs. Quantitative research uses data that are numerical and are based on the assumption that the numbers will describe a single reality. Statistics are often applied to find relationships between variables. Both quantitative and qualitative research are/or can be consistent with a basic or traditional scientific approach aimed at uncovering the relationship between vari- ables and factors involved in an implementation and learning outcomes.

The element of design in learning and educational research has been paid more attention recently. One of the traditional factors addressed is the extent to which an approach or design contributed to or inhibited outcomes. Previously, that aspect was addressed by formative evaluations. Recently, the quality of the design process itself has come under closer scrutiny. Design-based research and design method- ology are becoming more and more important for educational technology research and educational product development. The following sections will introduce the design-based research in details.

**The Concept of Design-Based Research**

Design-based research (DBR) was proposed as design experiments in articles by Brown and Collins. And now, it is a type of research methodology commonly used by researchers in the learning sciences. Design-based research is a systemic approach to the planning and implementing of innovations that emphasize an iterative approach to design with ongoing involvement collaboration with practitioners. DBR goes beyond formative evaluation research as the focus is on the rationale for design decisions and changes in the design as a technology-based learning effort evolves, although DBR can still be considered a kind of formative evaluation research.

The solutions that result from educational design research can be educational products (e.g., a multi-user virtual world learning game), processes (e.g., a strategy for scaffolding student learning in online courses), programs (e.g., a series of workshops intended to help teachers develop more effective questioning strategies), or policies (e.g., year-round schooling). Researchers attempt to solve significant real-world problems while at the same time they seek to discover new knowledge that can inform the work of others facing similar problems. Within design-based research methodology, interventions are conceptualized and then implemented iteratively in natural settings to test the ecological validity of the dominant theory and to generate new theories and frameworks for conceptualizing learning, instruction, design processes, and educational reform.

**Key Characteristics of DBR**

Design-based research exhibits the following characteristics: pragmatic, grounded, interventionist, iterative, collaborative, adaptive, and theory-oriented.

**Pragmatic:** it is concerned with generating usable knowledge and usable solu- tions to problems in practice.

**Grounded:** it uses theory, empirical findings, and craft wisdom to guide the work.

**Interventionist:** it is undertaken to make a change in a particular educational context.

**Iterative:** it evolves through multiple cycles of design, development, testing, and revision.

**Collaborative:** it requires the expertise of multi-disciplinary partnerships, including researchers and practitioners, but also often others (e.g., subject matter specialists, software programmers, or facilitators).

**Adaptive:** the intervention design and sometimes also the research design are often modified in accordance with emerging insights.

**Theory-oriented:** it uses theory to ground design, and the design and develop- ment work is undertaken to contribute to a broader scientific understanding.

**The Process of Design-Based Research**

The design-based research process has been described as iterative, as well as flexible. While multiple cycles of activity are clearly present across most models and frameworks, flexibility is present in all models. The generic model for conducting design-based research, and it contains these features:

- Three core phases in a flexible, iterative structure: analysis, design, and evaluation.
- Dual focus on theory and practice: integrated research and design processes; theoretical and practical outcomes.
- Indications of being use-inspired: planning for implementation and spread; interaction with practice; contextually responsive.

**Analysis and Exploration**

The first phase of design-based research is the analysis and exploration, which includes problem identification and diagnosis. As noted by Bannan-Ritland: "The first phase of design-based research is rooted in essential research steps of problem identification, literature survey, and problem definition" (p. 22). In line with the exploratory nature of design research, driving questions should, therefore, be open in nature. In this phase, people state problems through consultation with researchers and practitioners, analysis the research questions, and do a literature review.

The main products resulting from this phase are both practical and theoretical. From the practical perspective, this phase generates a clear understanding of the problem and its origins as well as specification of long-range goals. In addition, partial design requirements are determined by exploring the opportunities and boundary conditions present; and initial design propositions are generated based on contextual insights.

From the theoretical perspective, this phase produces a descriptive and analytical understanding of the given class of problems, as manifested in this case within a particular context.

**Design and Construction**

The second phase is design and construction, which is a coherent process followed and documented to arrive at a (tentative) solution to the problem. Unlike the other two main phases which follow empirical cycles based on a research chain of reasoning, the microcycle of design and construction resembles that of creating (not testing) a conceptual model.

Design refers to generate potential solutions to the problem, develop draft principles to guide the design of the intervention. Construction refers to the process of taking design ideas and applying them to actually manufacture the solution. This generally takes place through a prototyping approach, where successive approximations of the desired solution are created.The results of this phase are a research proposal, which includes details of the methodology of the intervention, implementation, and evaluation of the proposed solution, as it largely constitutes the data collection and analysis stages of the study. From the practical perspective, the intervention is conceived and assembled.From a theoretical perspective, the frameworks underpinning design as well as the justification for design decisions are articulated.

**Evaluation and Reflection**

The third phase is evaluation and reflection. Evaluation refers to the empirical testing that is done with a design or a constructed intervention (that is, the embodiments of design in the initial, partial, or final form.

Reflection involves active and thoughtful consideration of what has come together in both research and development (including theoretical inputs, empirical findings, and subjective reactions) with the aim of producing theoretical under- standing. Reflection is benefited most when approached through a combination of systematic and organic techniques.

The results of empirical findings, as well as critical reflection are then used to accept, refine, or refute the conjectures, frameworks, or principles that are portrayed in design documents (e.g., design frameworks) or embodied in actual (prototypes of) interventions.

**Interaction with Practice: Implementation and Spread**

The three core processes (analysis and exploration; design and construction; and evaluation and reflection) are interacting with practice through the (anticipation of) implementation and spread of interventions.

Researchers and practitioners jointly anticipate and plan for it from the very first stage of analysis and exploration, e.g., by tempering idealist goals with realistic assessments of what is possible; by taking practitioner concerns seriously; and by studying what intrinsic motives and natural opportunities are already present in the target setting.

This can include many kinds of professionals whose work relates to educational practice, such as teachers, administrators, teacher educators, examination agencies, inspectorates, policy makers, and textbook publishers. During analysis and explo- ration, this involvement is geared primarily toward clarifying the problem and shaping and understanding of constraints within which design will have to operate.Two Main

**Outputs**

In design-based research generic model, there are two main outputs: maturing interventions and theoretical understanding. Both outputs ripen over time and can be more locally relevant or more broadly applicable.

The intervention itself contributes directly to practice (by addressing the problem at hand) and indirectly to theoretical understanding (as one example of how specific, articulated, design frameworks can be reified). The theoretical under- standing is produced through (usually several) micro and/or mesocycles of design research.

The empirical findings and resulting conjectures provide important building blocks for theory, and can also contribute indirectly to practice as these ideas may be shared among professionals and used to build new interventions.

**DBR and Traditional Empirical Research**

Reeves draws a clear line between research conducted with traditional empirical goals and that inspired by development goals leading to "design principles.The traditional empirical research proposed the hypotheses based on observation and existing theories, which is tested by the design experiment. Then, the theory is refined based on the test results. Finally, practitioners apply the refinement theory. The cycle of traditional empirical research is the specification of new hypotheses.

The design-based research is based on the analysis of practical problems by researchers and practitioners in collaboration. Then, combine with the existing design principles and technology innovation to develop the solution, test and refine solutions iteratively in practice. Last, reflect the implementation of design principles and solutions. Design-based research is not for testing hypotheses, but for refining of problems, solutions, methods, and design principles.

**Case Study**

Different research reports are used here to illustrate the variety of educational design-based research conducted within the field of educational technology.

The first case is conducted, with substantial funding from the National Science Foundation and other sources. He put his efforts to refine a theory of transformational play while at the same time seeking to develop advanced forms of interactive learning games. It contains three qualitative studies focused on the challenges and successes involved in implementing Quest Atlantis, a 3D multi-player virtual environment (MUVE), which serves as the primary vehicle for instantiating Barab's transformational play learning theory and for allowing it to be refined through iterative design-based research.

The second case is co-led by an at-the-time early career assistant professor, Klopfer and Squire, with start-up funding from Microsoft and other sources. It is a multi-year project to enhance student learning related to environmental science through the development and refinement of learning games that are accessed with handheld devices such as PDAs and smart phones. In addition to developing an array of learning games, the project has sought to develop and refine a theoretical framework called "augmented reality educational gaming" that can be applied by other game designers. Meanwhile, it focuses on iterative design cycles based on five case studies conducted in real high school classrooms.

The third case is carried out by Oh, working with one other doctoral student and a practitioner with no funding beyond a graduate teaching assis- tantship. It pursued two primary goals: (1) optimizing collaborative group work in an online graduate-level course focused on "E-Learning Evaluation," and (2) developing a refined model of group work in online courses and identifying design principles for supporting online collaborative group work among adult learners. Oh use mixed methods to apply across several semester-length iterations of an online course to yield multiple distinct design principles for supporting group work by adults.

For each case, the problem addressed, the primary focus of the research, the intervention that was developed, the theoretical contributions, the methods used, and the scope of the intervention.

**Key Points in This Chapter**

1. Design-based research is a systemic approach to the planning and imple- menting of innovations that emphasize an iterative approach to design with ongoing involvement and collaboration with practitioners.
2. Design-based research exhibits the following characteristics: pragmatic, grounded, interventionist, iterative, collaborative, adaptive, and theory- oriented.
3. Three core phases of DBR include analysis and exploration, design and construction, evaluation and reflection.

# Research Analysis

**Introduction**

Design methodology is a powerful methodology for problem-forming and problem-solving which integrates human, business, and technological factors.Each designer wishes to work out preferable design; however, the innovative and practical products among the numerous products are just a rarity of the rarities. Designers need a thinking tool to help them master demands, develop divergent thinking, and arrange for product structure. Besides, they also need a design flow to make the design work structuralized, achieve a stable output, and improve work efficiency without omitting elements; they also need a work specification to accu- mulate and ensure quality and to coordinate between different designers.

In fact, according to the design characteristics of products, different industries have their own methodologies. For example, home furnishing design and graphic design have the universal design methods of the industry, to support for their design process. So does the Internet industry; during the Internet development history of more than 20 years, various companies form their respective design methods suitable for their respective demands.

The design methodology in this chapter summarizes the design experiences of various successful products and is the combination of experiences and skills extracted from multiple design works (including building design, industrial design, software design, and game design).

It is not only a kind of design thinking but also a set of feasible design flow, a complete and overall work specification. The design methodology guides designers to utilize the divergent thinking of the fragmentation and the method of exhaustion, to start from original demands, to conduct in-depth analysis on various design elements such as target user, stakeholders, competitive products, and scenes, and then screen, optimize, and output product functions and prototypes.

As a kind of thinking tool, the design methodology is applied to any design type work, including game designer, software designer, UI designer, management per- sonnel, or even administrative assistant. After the in-depth learning of methodol- ogy, they can master user demands, use scene, user pain spots during actual works, to work out better product or service.

**The Framework of Design Methodology**

The framework of design methodology. Firstly, design methodology based on original requirements, that is, there is a problem that needs to solve. The designers will analyze the target users related to this problem (or original demand), identify the characteristics of the target users from various dimensions, find out the stakeholders (broadly conceived to include learners, teachers, support personnel, and administrators) and their corresponding interests relevant to this problem. After analyzing the target users' demands and interests of the stakeholders, the designers can diversify, select, and improve their designs.

Next, specific to a particular industry and the potential product(s), designers will perform "competitive product analysis" and "scenario analysis" based on the original demand, which includes learning if there is any ready-made solution and what its vulnerabilities are and what can be improved. On the strength of the preliminary design, designers will build users' daily (no solutions) behavior sce- narios, mine user pain points, construct the various product application scenarios. In such a concrete process, the design is constantly improved to perfection.

Based on a full analysis of these aspects, designers will integrate a function list, or preliminary solution plan list aiming at the original demand. Finally, based on the "function list" and the original demand, the designers refer to the original demands again, consider the design purpose, and select the most proper and feasible solution to this demand.No matter what solution plan it is, as a designer, you should never forget to ask yourself: What kind of value does my solution plan (which can also be called the product) create for the user? Or what is the value proposition of this product? The whole process is a design process of focusing on problems, diverging problems, and focusing on problems again.

Under the ideal circumstances, this design process is a continuous, repeated, and endless problem-solving process. When thought of in this manner, design research is a kind of specialized formative evaluation effort.

**Original Requirements Analysis:Introduction to Original Requirements Analysis**

Original requirements refer to the unprocessed requirements or demands proposed by the originator at the launching stage of the project. It is the truthful description of the originator and product design requirements; it usually does not need modification.

Original requirements are the basis to direct designers to develop the design of products, and the scale to test whether the design complies with requirements. In the product design of designers, there is usually key information of each item that needs to be confirmed with the requirement originator, the proposition of the original requirement concept excellently solves the common problems such as the insuffi- ciency of communication and lack of information in design. Meanwhile, the original requirement marks the product expectation and design boundary and other contents of the original requirement, which is important and necessary for designers.

**General Process of Original Requirements Analysis**

Original requirements refer to the unprocessed needs or demands that are raised by the demand side in the beginning stage of the project.

Step 1: Obtain the original needs

Step 2: Systemize the original needs

Step 3: Extract the original needs

Step 4: Confirm the original needs

Original requirements usually are the unprocessed requirements acquired after a series of materials collection, and these materials can be research results or maybe meeting recordings, or the very words proposed directly by the originator. After acquiring the material list from the originator, the designer abstracts typically all unprocessed information one on one from the materials and come up with a copy of complete and structural original requirements and then deliver to the originator for signing and confirmation. After the originator confirms, the original requirements will be used as the direct basis for the subsequent product design.The original requirement is presented in a structured way, which the designer needs to abstract the information of every structure element from the product design requirement given by the requirement demand side.

Original requirements elements include originator, project name, required material list, original requirements description, target user, design purpose, usingOriginal Requirements Analysis 193

**The Websoft Case**

The chairman of the Websoft Company held a meeting with its CTO (Chief Technology Officer) to discuss the eye protection function of the student tablet. They determined what modules of functions this product should have, which aspects of design need more attention, and other core contents.After receiving the meeting recording, the designer analyzed and generated the information structuralized of the meeting recording into a piece of the original requirement Target User Analysis

**Introduction to Target User Analysis**

A target user is the intended audience or readership of publication, advertisement, or other messages. In marketing and advertising, it is a particular group of consumers within the predetermined target market, identified as the targets or recipients for a particular advertisement or message.

In product design, users of different ages, genders, and education may have different ideas on the same product and its operation. Therefore, in the process of product design, we should fully consider the users' various characteristics. Through target users' analysis, we can make clear the target groups of product and their needs. Analysis results for characteristics of users can be used as one of the bases to determine the direction of our product design and priority of requirements.

**The function of the target user analysis includes the following:**

- Clarify for whom the product is designed.
- Identify users' motive behind the needs.
- Provide a basis for prioritizing the product function design.

**The General Process of Target User Analysis**

The procedure of the target user analysis includes the following steps:

- Step 1: Analyze the target user according to the attribute tags listed.
- Step 2: Describe the attribute tags that may influence the product design and clarify the specific presentation of such an attribute tag.
- Step 3: Extract the design inspiration from the attribute description.

The attribute of the target user refers to the typical characteristics of the product users. Such attributes usually cover personal information, economy, culture, com- munity, hardware, software, characteristic, etc. Characteristic attribute refers to the values that the target user can generate for the design, which includes psychological characteristic attribute and behavior characteristic attribute.

There are many ways to analyze users, including interviews, live tracking, user-related personnel research, life experience simulation, viewing user analysis report on professional Web sites, reading books for relevant groups written by professionals and so on. One of the most common ways is to view online relevant information.hrough these methods,

we can understand target users more practically to extract accurately target users' attribute tags and prevent the designer from spec- ulating target user characteristics, to help us to design the product correctly.

**An Example of Target User Analysis**

The next step is the target user analysis for eye protection system, and the product of this analysis. In this product, target users are junior high and high school students, and we analyze their requirement features in many aspects, such as personalized requirements, prefer- ence culture, game awareness, vanity, self-control, study-induced stress, indepen- dent learning ability, mind of rivalry, sharing tendencies, rebellious, intensity with eyes, and eyesight protection awareness.

**Introduction of Stakeholder Analysis**

A stakeholder is a person such as an employee, customer, or citizen who is involved with an organization, society, etc. and therefore has responsibilities towards it and an interest in its success. Kaler defines stakeholders as those towards whom businesses owe moral duties and obligations beyond those generally owed to the general public. For example, sponsors, clients, users, partners, authority depart- ments, other interested persons, organizations, hardware/software influence, etc.

**Analysis of the stakeholders' influence on design will be conducted on the following aspects:**

- Clarify the design direction and design boundary.
- Extract the function needs or design inspiration.
- Specify the need priority and serve as a basis for judgment when there is any confliction.

**The General Process of Stakeholder Analysis**

Stakeholder analysis includes the three steps: to list stakeholders, to analyze the stakeholders, and to extract the function demands.

**List Stakeholders**

To analyze the stakeholders, we need to identify the right stakeholders and ensure that no important stakeholders are omitted. The fragmentation method and the exhaustive method will serve as the two important methods for identifying important stakeholders. We can identify the required stakeholders in the following reference:

- Identifying the stakeholders from the main product scenario or customer process.
- Identifying the stakeholders in the product life circle.
- Identifying stakeholders by searching the keywords.

### Analyze the Stakeholders

The stakeholders involved in a product are multiple. We can identify and categorize the stakeholders and determine the roles they are playing in a project so that we can catch a structured and logic analysis of the stakeholders.

we will classify the stakeholders in several main dimensions such as the con- tributor, the customer, the user, the authority department, the partner, other parties interested (software and hardware shall also be considered in certain cases).

Then, we will determine the importance of stakeholders through identifying the demands, expectations, contributions, functions of the stakeholders on the program, and prioritize the stakeholders based on their power, influence, attitude, urgency.Last, we will analyze stakeholders' interest and demands.

### Extract the Function Demands

Based on the analysis of the stakeholders' project interests, negative impact, expectations/requirements, and objectives/motivation, we can identify the stake- holder's pain points and quick points, get inspirations, and provide the basis for product design.Design inspiration can be product use scenario, product function, or certain characteristics, etc. At this stage, the content of the design is entirely kept to extract a variety of feasible solutions.

### An Example of Stakeholder Analysis

Based on the analysis on the stakeholders' project interests, negative impact, expectations/requirements, and objectives/motivation, we can identify the stake- holder's pain points and quick points, get inspirations, and provide the basis for product design. Table is an example of design inspiration from analyzing main stakeholders of the takeout platform.

### Competitor Analysis :Introduction to Competitor Analysis

Competitors are defined as firms offering products or services that are close substitutes, in the sense that they serve the same customer.

### Design Methodology

Competitive product analysis, in essence, is a "comparative study" originating from anthropology. It is a qualitative research method that studies user behavior. Firstly, it requires finding out the similar phenomenon or things; secondly, the same phenomena or things are grouped and tabled for comparison; thirdly, conduct further analysis on the comparing results. Its main purpose is to provide references on functionality, usability, key technologies for product design, to help designers to explore the core demands of the target users, and learn how competitive products meet the requirements of the target users.

There are three types of competitors:

- Competitors with identical functions: products that can perform the same function with the target product, and are highly correspondent to the original needs and on the same platform with the target product (Web, desktop, mobile terminal).
- Competitors with similar core functions: products that can perform the same or similar function with the target product, and are highly correspondent to the original needs and on the same platform with the target product (Web, desktop, mobile terminal).
- Competitors with the same-essence function: competitive products that have different realizing channels or forms but can perform the same function with the target product. Such products are usually goods or services with reference values.

### General Process of Competitor Analysis

Competitive product analysis includes the following process:

1. Competitive products collection: Collect competitive products as many as possible through all available channels;
2. Competitive products selection: Classify and select the core competitive products worthy of reference from the available competitive products;

3. Competitive products dismantling and function integration: Dismantle and analyze the core competitive products to understand the motivation behind the design function of competitive products. Identify the excellent design and integrate it into their products.

### Competitive Product Collection

Competitive product collection refers to the process to get more referential products through various methods. Analysis of competitive products can contribute to our product design. Under the premise to stick to the core demands of the target user, find more things that can meet the core demands.Take chat apps as an example. Its core demand is to satisfy the communication demands between people. In addition to QQ, WeChat, Skype, telephone, SMS, e-mail, and even sign language can be used to meet the users' communication demands. Therefore, these products are listed in our competitive products.

**Competitive products collecting method is as follows:**

1. Find the right competitive products from app market, professional Web sites, and industrial investigation reports;
2. Use a search engine, such as Google, Baidu, and Yahoo to find the right competitive products;
3. User interview: interview the target users to find the right competitive products;
4. Think if there are any other ways to realize the core functions, such as products of the software, materials, services;
5. Expand part of the functions: Certain functions can be enlarged to find the right competitive products, such as expanding from buying cinema tickets to buying tickets
6. Other industries: Analyze how other industries make achievements. For example, consider how the financial industry achieves success when devel- oping a calculator for the education industry.
7. Others: through fragmentation and operation related method to find compet- itive products.
8. Extract keywords based on the key stakeholder analysis and then collect competitive products.

### Competitive Products Selection

In the actual work, we divide the selected competitive product into three categories based on the product functions, match degree, and realization method. In principle, all competitive products can be classified into one of the three categories:

1. Competitive products with the same functions: Competitive products are those which can reach the desired targets and share the same platform (Web, desktop, mobile terminal) with our designed software.
2. Competitive products with similar functions: Competitive products are those which have the same or similar functions and part of their functions conforms to the requirements and shares a different platform (Web, desktop, mobile terminal) with our designed software.
3. Competitive products which have essentially the same function: referring to competitive products that have different realizing channels or forms but can perform the same function with the target product. Such products are usually goods or services with reference values.

### Competitive Product Dismantling

Competitive product dismantling is to dismantle competitive products in a frag- mentation manner. In simple terms, it is to experience competitive products, get the functions, record the whole process, and make notes for the contents displayed through the dismantling template. We divide the dismantling into three steps: select competitive products to be dismantled, dismantle competitive products, label dismantling method and add function notes.

### Competitive Product Function Integration

Competitive product function integration refers to the collection and integration of all the functions of the disassembled competitive product, and the marking of the importance degree of each of them by analysis.After the disassembly of all competitive products, integrate functions of each competitive product according to "List for

Disassembly of Competitive Products." Generally speaking, three levels are reserved for each competitive product: func- tional modules, the first level of functions and the second level of functions, and the "List for Functional Integration of Competitive Products," formed finally.

### An Example for Competitive Product Analysis

Take the eye use protective system as the example, Appendix 1 is competitive product selection, Appendix 2 is competitive product function disassembly, and Appendix 3 is competitive product functional integration of the eye use protective system.

### Scenario Analysis:Introduction of Scenario Analysis

Scenario refers to the situation which the user may encounter in using or getting in touch with the products, including the operation process and feelings.

Scenario analysis is a process of analyzing possible future events by considering alternative possible outcomes (sometimes called "alternative worlds"). Thus, the scenario analysis, which is a main method of projections, does not try to show one exact picture of the future. Instead, it presents consciously several alternative future developments.

### General Process of Scenario Analysis

Generally speaking, the flow of scenario analysis is as follows:

1. Firstly, it is the listing of elements, and the thinking mode of exhaustion shall be utilized to try to list all the elements related to the product; scenario elements may include time, place, participants, cause, process, tools, application conditions, etc. Secondly, combine elements one by one according to the listed scenario elements, to describe a general situation of the scenario.
2. Thirdly, conduct scenario description, i.e., show the behavioral process of users with clear, detailed, and careful flow description. After the process of scenario title and scenario description, we need to mine and summarize pain points and pleasant points of users.
3. Finally, aiming at the detected user pain points or pleasant points, we shall give corresponding functions or solutions. The whole flow is summarized as five pro- cedures: list of elements, scenario title, scenario description, seeking pain point/pleasant points, and giving solutions.

### An Example of Scenario Analysis

The scenario analysis for eye use protective system is shown in Appendix, and the scenario description and function extraction.

### Function List

Function list is the integration of functions that is designed to satisfy certain demands, which also includes the correlation, level of importance, and remarks of the functions. It may be the documents that contain tables, mind maps that can display the relationship between functions.

In "Design Methodology," it is needed to take competitive product function integration result as the framework and blueprint on the basis of considering the core value of the product and acquiring the basic structure of the product, and in combination of the functions acquired from the nodes such as original demand, analysis on stakeholder, analysis on target users, scenario analysis, to form the product function list.

### The General Process of Function List

Generally speaking, the output of the function list contains the following procedures:

1. Reinspect the original demand and sort out the preliminary list
2. Expand the optional schemes and conduct self-inspection to function list
3. Make clear the core functions and classify and sort out functions
4. Conduct screening on function list and rank for function priority
5. Supplement function description and check on function list
6. Books of research of fuction list

**The above procedures can be divided into function integration and function list manufacture:**

1. Function integration is conducted in order to maximize the optional schemes, and it is necessary for the designers to think about the type of functions, the origin of them, and the arrangement structure of them;
2. Function list manufacture is the procedure for the determination of the final solution, and it is necessary for designers to think of what functions shall be reserved, and what functions are important, and whether the functions are clearly described, etc.

**For the final function list, the following procedures could be followed to finish the function.**

1. Step 1: Trim functions. Function classification is to classify all the functions of a product, clarifying the function modules, eliminating or correcting the unnecessary functions, etc.
2. Step 2: Mark the level of importance. The level of importance for the product functions can be divided into four categories: necessary, suggested, better with, and not suggested. Evaluate the design satisfaction level of the product based on the review of original needs and analyses of stakeholders, com- petitors, and scenarios. Assume the first version of WhatsApp is to be developed, the necessary functions include registration (bound to phone numbers), dialogue, communication by phones while the suggested functions include portrait, iCloud backup, broadcast, groups, message-receiving confirmation.
3. Step 3: Remarks. Enter the reflections on the functions and solutions, including any items deemed to be specified by the designer

### Extended Reading

Approaches to delivering design methodology vary in terminology and phases of execution. The UK design council illustrates a four-stage process: discover, define, develop, and deliver termed the "Double Diamond" (Design Council), whereas innovation consultancy IDEO proposes the approach incorporating three spaces: inspiration, ideation, and implementation.

### Double Diamond

This double diverge-converge pattern was first introduced in 2005 by the British Design Council, which called it the double diamond design process model. The Design Council divided the design process into four stages: "discover" and "define"—for the divergence and convergence phases of finding the right problem, and "develop" and "deliver"—for the divergence and convergence phases of finding the right solution.

### Design Thinking for Educators (IDEO)

IDEO (pronounced "eye-dee-oh") is an international design and consulting firm founded in Palo Alto, California, in 1991. The company uses the design thinking methodology to design products, services, environments, and digital experiences. Additionally, the company has become increasingly involved in management consulting and organizational design.

The design process is what puts design thinking into action. It is a structured approach to generating and evolving ideas. It has five phases that help navigate the development from identifying a design challenge to finding and building a solution, which contains discovery, interpretation, ideation, experimentation, and evolution. It is a deeply human approach that relies on your ability to be intuitive, to interpret what you observe and to develop ideas that are emotionally meaningful to those you are designing for—all skills you are well-versed in as an educator.

### Key Points in This Chapter

1. Design methodology is a powerful methodology for innovation has emerged, which integrates human, business, and technological factors in problem-forming, solving, and design
2. The framework of design methodology: First, design methodology is based on original requirements or problems; then designers will perform "competitive product analysis," "scenario analysis," "target user analysis," "stakeholder analysis" based on the original demand; after that, designers will integrate a function list; finally,

designers will select the most proper and feasible solution to the demand.

# Works Of Research Technology

**Introduction**

It is obviously true that educational technology changes, and that changes are happening at an accelerating pace. The challenge is to make effective use of new technologies in different learning scenarios in the twenty-first century. In this chapter, four kinds of technologies will be discussed: learning analytics, artificial intelligence, adaptive technologies, and wearable devices. These chosen technolo- gies in each of these four areas are changing and likely to continue to change and evolve for some time. It should be noticed that a technology need not be a specific device, as a technology could be generally understood to be a systematic and disciplined application of knowledge. Implementation issues and the likely impact on learning and instruction of these emerging technologies are also addressed in this chapter.

**Emerging Technologies**

Technologies have changed and continue to change education. For example, social networking and digital conferencing have helped improve student teacher and student student relationships and collaborative learning in some cases. Digital game technologies and interactive simulations have also helped make some learning situations more effective and engaged. In this chapter, we focus on the four kinds of technologies that have demonstrated their potentials to improve learning and instruction: learning analytics, artificial intelligence, wearable devices, and adaptive learning.

**Learning Analytics**

In some sectors, the relatively recent emergence of big data and analytics is now viewed as having the potential to transform economies and increase organizational productivity. Learning analytics is the measurement, col- lection, analysis, and reporting of data about learners and their contexts for under- standing and optimizing learning and the environments in which learning occurs. Unfortunately, educational systems primary, secondary, and postsecondary have made limited use of the available data to improve teaching, learning, and learner success. Despite the field of education lagging behind other sectors, there has been an explosion of interest in analytics as a solution for many current challenges, such as retention and learner support . For example, a learning dashboard overview learning data through data visualization tools much of the software that is currently used for learning analytics.

**Artificial Intelligence**

Artificial intelligence (AI; also called machine intelligence or MI) is intelligent problem-solving behavior displayed by machines in contrast with the natural intelligence displayed by humans and other animals. In computer science, AI research focuses on the study of intelligent agents, which are devices that can perceive a situation or environment and take actions that maximize the chance of success in attaining a goal, and the goal may be determined by a person or gen- erated by a system in the case of higher order AI agents. The traditional problem areas of AI research include problem-solving, complex reasoning, knowledge extraction and representation, planning, learning new rules and concepts, natural language processing, and the ability to move and manipulate objects. AI is a branch of computer science that attempts to understand the nature of intelligent behavior to design and create devices that perform in ways that are similar to how an informed human would perform in that situation. AI research and development areas include robotics, spoken language recognition, image recogni- tion, natural language processing, and expert systems to support decision making and problem solving. Artificial intelligence can simulate the information process of human consciousness and thinking. Artificial intelligence is not human intelligence, but it can think like people, and it may surpass people's intelligence.

**Wearable Devices**

Wearable technology refers to computer-based devices that can be worn by users, taking the form of an accessory such as jewelry, eyewear, or even actual items of clothing such as shoes or a jacket. The advantage of wearable technology is that it can easily integrate tools to track sleep, movement, location, and social media interactions. In the case of Oculus Rift and other VR headsets, wearable devices can support virtual realities. There are even new classes of devices that are seamlessly integrated with a user's everyday life and movements. New smartwatches from Apple, Garmon, Samsung, Sony, and Pebble are already allowing users to check e-mails and perform other productive tasks through a small interface. Thanks to the quantified-self movement, today's wearables not only track where a person goes, what a person does, and how much time spent on doing something, but now what a person's aspirations are and when or where those can be accomplished. Some popular wearable devices are bracelets such as Huawei Talk Band 2 and Xiaomi Mi Band track move- ment, exercise, and other health-related activities. There are tremendous implica- tions for physical education, nutrition, and health classes in K-12 education.

**Adaptive Learning**

Adaptive learning technologies refer to software and online devices and environ- ments that adjust to individual needs. The start of the work on adaptive and intelligent learning systems is usually traced back to the SCHOLAR intelligent tutoring system that offered adaptive learning for the topic of the geography of South America. Adaptive learning is a sophisticated, data-driven, and in some cases, nonlinear approach to instruction and remediation, adjusting to a learner's interactions and demonstrated performance level, and subsequently anticipating what types of content and resources learners need at a specific point in time to make progress. In this sense, contemporary educational tools are now capable of learning the way people learn. Adaptive devices are enabled by machine learning technologies that develop a rich profile of the learner including prior knowledge and interests. Adaptive devices can adapt to each student's progress and interests and adjust content in real time as well as customize exercises appropriate for a specific learner. Many educators envision these adaptive platforms as tutors that can provide per- sonalized instruction on a large scale. Currently, several systems and platforms providing adaptation to users' learning styles, cognitive abilities, affective states, and the context of the learning have been created. In addition, many of the adaptive learning systems that incorporate learning styles are based on the notion that matching the learning strategies with the learning styles can improve learner performance; examples include MANIC. MANIC is a Web-based instructional system which provides lecture-based material. In MANIC, the adaptation is achieved by providing different media representations for each learner.

**Diffusion of Innovations.**

Diffusion of innovations is a theory that aims to clarify how, why, and at what rate new ideas and technology spread. In Everett Rogers's book Diffusion of Innovations, which was first published in 1962 and is now in its fifth edition, Rogers claims that diffusion is the process by which an innovation is com- municated over time among the participants in a social system. The beginning of the Diffusion of Innovations theory is diverse and spanning many disciplines.Diffusion occurs through a five-step decision-making process. It occurs through a series of communication channels over a period of time among the members of a similar social system. Rogers' five stages (steps): awareness, interest, evaluation, trial, and adoption are integral to this theory. Diffusion of Innovations has been applied to numerous contexts, such as technology promotion with a particularly large impact on the use of technology.

**Issues Involving in Emerging Technologies**

Over the past decade, there has been an emphasis on equal access to information and communications technologies. Lack of equal access is often referred to regarding a divide between those in developed countries and regions and those in less developed countries or between the well-to-do and the poor. To benefit from new technologies, one must have access and the means to gain access to the Internet and other resources, which is an essential and persistent concern. Other issues related to new technologies concern privacy, ethics, and security. In addition to these human-oriented issues, there are a number of implementation issues that need to be addressed, including accreditation, scalability, sustainability as well as issues that are specific to specific regions and cultures (e.g., humor, color, and examples do not always work well in different cultural contexts).

**Ethical, Security and Privacy Issues**

Ethical, security, and privacy issues cover a family of things that have importance in everyday life. Ethics in technology is a sub-field of ethics addressing the ethical questions specific to the use of technology to support learning and instruction. The ethics involved in the development of new technology—whether it is always, never, or contextually right or wrong to invent and implement a technological innovation. Ethics relates to the question of what is right or wrong regarding technology use in learning proposed an educratic oath for educators, and the first part of that oath is to do no harm to learners. Disadvantaging some learners when using technology can widen the digital divide and is a violation of that principle.Security is a key to technology use in education. The use of student data is crucial for personalized learning and continuous improvement, but using student data to create security issues. Security, acting as the stewards of student data, presents educators with several responsibilities. School officials, families, and software developers have to be mindful of how data privacy, confidentiality, and security practices affect students. Schools and districts have an obligation to tell students and families what kind of student data the school or third parties (e.g., online educational service providers) are collecting and how the data can be used. Privacy is a particularly hot-button issue in technology, considering the perva- sive nature of the Internet in people's daily lives. Many Web sites collect user data, from usernames and passwords to personal information such as addresses and phone numbers, without the explicit permission of users. Selling this information is widely considered unethical, but is often in a legal gray area because the user provides the data in the first place.

### Quality Control, Accreditation and Sustainability Issues

Accreditation and Quality Assurance has established itself as the leading infor- mation and discussion forum for all aspects relevant to quality, transparency, and reliability of measurement. Since the 1990s, with the rapid development and popularization of the Internet, a wide range of resources cooperation and sharing has become the general trend, and the technical standards of learning resources in this process have played a crucial role.These issues involve resources sharing and relevant standards making in dif- ferent countries which will affect the diffusion of technology. For example, SCORM, which defines communications between client-side content and a host system are closely related to sustainability.For sustainability, once the resources cooperation and sharing process have been fully implemented, efforts must turn to greater efficiency in programme delivery and to maintaining stakeholder engagement, and also political support for widescale realignment of budgets and resources. Even initially effective, resources coopera- tion, and sharing interventions may change in their effects over time. Therefore, interventions must adapt to changing circumstances and contexts over time to continue to be effective and relevant to stakeholders and intended target groups.

### Culture and Regional Issues

The utilization of technology has a close relationship to specific regions and cul- tures. Culture and region may affect the transfer of technology. New groups of students from different backgrounds should be considered. Some are digital natives (persons who understand the value of digital technology and seek out every opportunity to use it), whereas some may be digital immigrants reluctant adopters. The dif- ferent generations with different cultural and regional backgrounds may have a different understanding of technology and its use in a lesson.Culture and regional differences affect human behavior patterns, and these differences are always reflected in the way people study, share knowledge and skills with others, and so on. Some researchers hold the view that cultural differences can have a negative effect on students' participation in online courses.

### Challenges for Educational Technology

In addition to the issues previously discussed, there are a number of recurring problem areas that have been called challenges. That report focused on the role and impact of computing and technology in education, including rec- ommendations for the future. Seven grand challenges were identified followed by seven technology recommendations, which will be discussed in the following texts. In addition, the New Media Consortium's *Horizon Reports* emphasize similar challenges and considerations.

### Personalizing Education

The one-method-fits-all approach does not match up with a diverse population and the potential of new technologies; moreover, finding in cognitive psychology and new technologies makes it possible to create effective learning activities to meet individual student needs and interests.

### Assessing Student Learning

There is a need for effective assessments of students and teachers, not only for accountability and promotion (summative) but also to improve learning and instruction (formative). The focus of assessment should be on improving learning, and assessments should be seamless and ubiquitous (woven into learning activities unobtrusively), especially from the perspective of life-long learning.

### Supporting Social Learning

Supporting meaningful and collaborative learning activities is more important than ever before, partly due to requirements in the workplace to work collaboratively and partly due to the affordances of new Web 2.0 technologies.

### Diminishing Boundaries

Traditional boundaries between students and teachers, between and among personal abilities and types of learning, between formal and informal learning, and between learning and working are changing and becoming blurred in the twenty-first cen- tury; this creates a need to recognize the significance of informal learning and different learner abilities and interests.

### Developing Alternative Teaching Strategies

The teacher is no longer the sole source of expertise in classroom settings due to the widespread availability of networked resources; this creates a need to change instructional approaches and train teachers accordingly.

### Enhancing the Role of Stakeholders

Stakeholders in educational systems need to develop trust that those systems are adequately preparing students for productive lives in twenty-first-century society; as a consequence, there is a need to regularly consult with employers, parents, administrators, teachers, and students to ensure that all stakeholders have confi- dence that the educational system is working well.

### Addressing Policy Changes

The knowledge society requires flexibility on the part of an informed population; educational inequities and the digital divide can challenge the stability of a society and need to be addressed, as with the other challenges.

### Challenges in Horizon Reports

The Horizon Project defines solvable challenges, difficult challenges, and wicked challenges. Solvable challenges that we understand and know how to solve including improving digital literacy and integrating formal and informal learning. Difficult challenges are ones that we understand but for which solutions are elusive, such as achievement gap and advancing digital equity. Wicked challenges are categorized as complex to even define, much less address, such as managing knowledge obsolescence and rethinking the roles of educators.

### Key Points in This Chapter

1. Four kinds of emerging technologies will have potentials to improve learning and instruction: learning analytics, artificial intelligence, wearable devices, and adaptive learning.
2. Issues involving in emerging technologies: ethical, security and privacy issues, quality control, accreditation and sustainability issues, culture and regional issues.

Challenges for educational technology: personalizing education, assessing student learning, supporting social learning, diminishing boundaries, devel- oping alternative teaching strategies, enhancing the role of stakeholders, addressing policy changes, challenges in Horizon Reports.

www.ingramcontent.com/pod-product-compliance
Lightning Source LLC
Chambersburg PA
CBHW060118120726
48003CB00009B/2686